Aspects of Thérèse

Bruce Stewart

Aspects of Thérèse

Thérèse of Lisieux, Little White Flower
and Doctor of the Church

ST PAULS

ST PAULS
Morpeth Terrace, London SW1P 1EP, United Kingdom
Maynooth, Co. Kildare, Ireland

© ST PAULS (UK) 1997

ISBN 085439 524 5

Set by TuKan, High Wycombe
Produced in the EU
Printed by The Guernsey Press Co. Ltd, Guernsey, C.I.

ST PAULS is an activity of the priests and brothers of the
Society of St Paul who proclaim the Gospel through the media
of social communication

Contents

Foreword   7

1. Thérèse and the Pursuit of Pleasure   17

2. Thérèse and Love   37

3. Thérèse and the Job in Hand   57

4. Thérèse and the Social Dimension   79

5. Thérèse and the He and the She of it   103

6. Thérèse and Authority   127

7. Thérèse and the Grim Reaper   149

Foreword

$\mathcal{I}$ was baptised a Catholic by an old German Marist in New Zealand called Fr Condringer. Thérèse of Lisieux, or 'the Little Flower' as she is more familiarly known, had only recently been canonised a saint. A plaster statue of her adorned his bush church. She smiled wanly from behind a jungle of silver fern, fired up by pohutakawa blossom or wild kowhai in season. Pious nuns kept the forest flowering.

Halfway through the christening, Condringer broke off the guttural rush of his Latin – priests of the time always took the liturgy at an Indianapolis Trials rate – to whisper to my mother: 'I will dedicate your new baby to our new saint'.

My mother, an unsophisticated Irishwoman, took this to mean something very special indeed. Ever afterwards she spoke of it to me in hushed tones. For my part I grew up thinking 'dedication' was some kind of solemn Catholic rite, reserved to the very few. I noticed that books I read were sometimes 'dedicated' to people, usually because they had somehow helped with the writing. That didn't make a lot of sense. To the best of my knowledge, the Little Flower had had nothing to do with my infliction upon the human race.

I was virtually adult before I found out the term 'dedication' was utterly meaningless. What Condringer meant by his aside to my mother we shall probably now never know, but the most likely explanation is that he gave me Thérèse's name. Priests used often to mutter the name of a favourite saint under their breath when the parents had opted for Melvin or Hazel. The sex of the baby was immaterial. You needed the handle of someone securely in the heavenly band to get baptised at all, so it was less important who the saint was than that the name of a saint should be there. As is well known, there is as yet no St Bruce.

I knew little more of Thérèse until my teenage years. Her statue smiled and smiled from the ecclesiastical wildwood and that was all. Then I read her autobiography, *L'Histoire d'une Ame*. It at once made me want to throw up. It was basically the story of her childhood in nineteenth century Normandy, her admission to the Carmel of Lisieux at the early age of 15, the events leading up to her premature death when she was only 24: but there was a simpering, teesy-weesy quality to the writing that put me in mind of little girls at primary school who had studied elocution, and could not be prevented from getting up and reciting poems about trolls and princesses. (Oddly enough, the young Thérèse had been good at that too, inflicting fairytales she made up as she went along on a captive audience in the school playground.)

L'Histoire d'une Ame was subtitled *The Story of a Little White Flower*, and that about summed it up for me. By page 3 we were strolling in green pastures by the cool water's brink and speculating on what a wild flower would say if it could talk and Jesus picked it. After that I would not have been in the least surprised to read that a baby was born every time a guardian angel blew its vigilant nose.

And yet this same author of juvenile twaddle, I was reliably informed, was one of the most significant and spiritually advanced saints of modern times.

It was a bit of a mystery. Given the additional puzzle of the 'dedication', I felt somehow involved, and as time went by slowly but surely became preoccupied with Thérèse. As with the little girls smothered in elocution at primary school, I began to ask myself if there really was a person hidden behind the big bow and the ill-chosen material.

Strangely, they were asking the same question in Rome. The grave deliberations which would result in John Paul II's 1997 declaration of Thérèse as a Doctor of the Church were already under way. Learned theologians and solemn Cardinals were turning from knotty problems like Grace and Free Will and Law and Liberation to speculations about flowers and woods and brooks, and the catching of butterflies for the greater glory of God.

One must make a comment in passing here.

Nobody, I think, would have been more surprised than Thérèse herself by all this. She was the least self-regarding of persons. To find herself up there with Basil and Augustine and Thomas Aquinas would have shocked her rigid. A pathologically shy Little Flower at the best of times, she would have shuddered on her stem and bent hopelessly before the wind. As we shall see later, she believed herself critically outranked by anyone in the Church who could *think*.

But as for me, I began to discover someone I had not expected behind the vomitous imagery: a shrewd, disarmingly direct individual, of identifiable gender but uncertain *genre*. She certainly merited further scrutiny. In a sense, this book is the fruit of that investigation, many years on. It has never really stopped. I unfailingly home in on the next half-baked article about Thérèse in the religious press, the next turgid pamphlet in the church rack. Aspects of Thérèse beckon to me, compel me, haunt my mind.

The fascinating thing about her is that she is not only one of the most significant saints of modern times, she has also been one of the most popular. An astonishingly wide range of people, religious or non-religious, it seems not to matter, have been attracted to Thérèse of Lisieux. Yet attitudes have changed enormously in the hundred years since her death. It is perhaps worth asking as the twentyfirst century looms if she still holds up as a model and exemplar in a secularist society. In her disillusioned and positivistic centenary year, is there anyone left who actually needs a Little Flower?

The facts of Thérèse's life are probably widely enough known, but it will be as well to rehearse them here. Louis Martin, her father, was a watchmaker and jeweller of Alencon, and then of Lisieux. He did well out of his affluent clients, and achieved modest investments and property. His wife Zelie was a craftswoman of *Point d'Alencon*. She was apparently highly skilled, and a demand for her lacemaking continued long into her married life. She bore Louis nine children, four of whom died, Thérèse being the lastborn in 1873. Then, when Thérèse was only five, Zelie contracted an early cancer and died too.

It was naturally a devastating blow to the family. Yet of the Martin children who survived, all girls, the entire five became nuns. This must be some sort of Catholic record. But the Martin girls broke even that, for four of the five became nuns at precisely the same convent, the Carmel of Lisieux. Aged Carmelites went to their graves lamenting that their ancient and holy Order (allegedly dating back to Old Testament times, to the prophet Elijah, no less) was being taken over by a group of sharp little provincial opportunists.

Thérèse's sisters were Marie, Pauline, Léonie and Céline. Marie, the eldest, was separated from Thérèse by 13 years. After Zelie's death, Louis became something of a recluse. When all bar Céline had gone off to the convent, he suffered a stroke. This led to a mental collapse, and he had to go into a home. Here he perished in 1894. Thérèse – by an irony, for she had been his youngest – barely outlived him, dying of consumption in 1897, three months before her 25th birthday. She had completed *L'Histoire d'une Ame* just two weeks before she died.

She was canonised a saint in 1925. That must have come as something of a surprise to her sisters, otherwise still living out predictably dull lives as religious. (Céline survived longest, dying as late as 1959.) It is practically unheard of for a 'confessor' – i.e., a non-martyr – to be raised to the Church's altars so soon after her death, or within the lifetime of her siblings. There would hardly seem time for the Devil's Advocate to have got his act together. It seems *L'Histoire d'une Ame*, precious, syrupy, garrulous, direly romantic when it is not being merely pedestrian, was more than partly responsible.

L'Histoire is the only thing Thérèse ever wrote, apart from a clutch of devotional poems and a lot of letters. It emerged out of a conversation around the winter fire in the recreation room of the Carmel of Lisieux in 1895. You had to go in there if you wanted to be half-way warm, because the rest of the old convent was cruelly damp and unheated. Thérèse had been talking of incidents in her childhood, of which she seemed to have total recall, and Marie (then Sr Marie of the Sacred Heart) said to Pauline (then Reverend Mother Agnes of Jesus, the superior: oh yes, the Martin girls were moving in on Carmel all right) 'Oh, what a pity all this cannot be written down for us! If you were to ask Sr Thérèse of the Child Jesus to write down her childhood memories, Mother, how much pleasure it would give us.' Thérèse gave a small snort of laughter at that, but Pauline gravely said 'I order you to write down the memories of your childhood.'

The stickily pious like to murmur that this 'command' indicated the Holy Spirit at work, or anyway something other than beetles moving in the woodwork. It is certainly most unusual for a Superior in religious life to 'order' a subject to do anything. Given the vow of obedience, it puts the subject under an obligation in conscience, and that normally is not done without a compelling reason. However, Thérèse bowed before the formality, and the autobiography was composed in three parts.

The first part is Thérèse's immediate response to Pauline's order, and comprises about half the book as it reads now. It was written, mainly in Thérèse's spare time and a crabbed hand, from January 1895 to January 1896. The second part is really just a long letter to Marie, written in response to her request that Thérèse should add something about her 'spiritual discoveries'. (The 'Little Way', about which we shall hear a great deal as we proceed.) Then when Thérèse was ill, the new Prioress, a certain (rather formidable) Mother Marie de Gonzague, at Pauline's suggestion asked Thérèse to insert a final section about her life as a religious. The result was the third part of the autobiography, written in a cheap notebook in June of 1897, and in pencil, because Thérèse was by that time too weak to hold a pen.

A month later she was dead. The Carmel of Lisieux then found itself stuck with a manuscript that it did not really know what to do with. A certain Dom Madelaine, prior of the Abbey of Mondaye, read it and found it basically edifying. He thus did some editing on it, and it was published in a limited edition, being distributed to sister Carmelite houses. (Ironically, they didn't like it much: teaching one's grandmother to suck eggs, it seemed to be thought, and who on earth were these people the authoress fails to name but notes as being dreadfully hard to get along with?) But then the general public somehow got hold of it, and it took off like a rocket. There had to be urgent and repeated reprints of what was seized upon first of all as a moving devotional text, then as an inspirational life story, eventually a spiritual classic.

But it remains a callow, kittenish document, bursting with *gaucherie* and embarrassing sentimentality. This is not to pretend of that it does not also contain profundities, insights, unexpected perceptions, and a lot of horse sense. Thérèse is not now hailed as a doctor, or teacher, of the Church for nothing. It is exactly like the naive, sensitive, immature, stubborn, out of touch, right-on young woman who brought it into being.

All for Jesus with a smile, was the horrendous motto of Thomas Merton's unbearable abbot. Well, there is honey still for tea, Thérèse assures us, even though of course we may be suffering too much to be able to swallow it. If you want to be holy, just be a toy that the Divine Child can play with or kick into a corner as he chooses. God made the rose in its glory, the lily in its whiteness, but he equally loves the violet with its sweet smell, the daisy in its charming simplicity.

Yes, pack the Quells and the Dramamine. Bring along the games and puzzles to make the journey tolerable. Hush, hush, whisper who dares. Noddy and Big Ears are saying their prayers.

1.

Thérèse

and the

Pursuit of Pleasure

For most people, saints are natural-born crepe-hangers. Their haloes may sparkle brighter than the lights of Las Vegas, but they are hardly the sort to let their hair down and pop a cork, or beam jolly assent when others do.

There is a story in Rodriguez, that old Jesuit dominie, about a monk in an early desert community who fasted on bread and water all Lent long, and then when Easter came would not give up his dreary penance. While the other monks thus got stuck into double portions of lentils (or whatever it was the Fathers of the Desert hollered for when it was party time), our dogged saint persisted with his maceration. Yet as the evening of Easter Day drew in, an unearthly scream was heard to echo throughout the pious community. The bread-and-water fiend had hurled himself from his cell high on a cliff, with a singular suitability breaking his stiff neck on the rocks below.

Ah yes, you may nod sagely: we have been there before with Aesop. But Rodriguez for his part simply observes that despite enviable holiness of life, the monk had failed to extirpate pride from his heart. That was his failing. To continue to deprive yourself of the starchy foods, therefore, even when Lent has belly-rumbled its way into a more indulgent season, remains a holy and wholesome thing to do. We are not put on this earth to cosset ourselves. But motivation is a tricky commodity, and you need to get it dead right, or you too could finish up deprived of Christian burial.

There is of course Manichaeism deep in all this. But then there always has been in the saintly approach to pleasure and its regulation. Anchorites or common or garden monks have always found it difficult to distinguish between Christian asceticism and what may be seen as heretical hatred of matter. There was another old Father of the Desert who, wishing to pray rather than sleep at night, tied his long hair to a nail in the wall, so that when the weakness of nature caused him to drop off, he could be rudely jerked back to his spiritual duties. You can't get much closer to contempt for the body and its demands than that.

The notion seems to have been essentially that you cut yourself off from anything you liked. Penance was never represented as an end in itself, but there was certainly the underlying suggestion that cracking hardy was more virtuous than indulging human frailty. It was still very much that way as late as my childhood in the 1930s. 'She's very holy,' my Irish mother would whisper of a devout lady in the parish. 'She weighs her food in Lent.' If you were halfway pious, you would leap out of bed for 6 a.m. Mass of a Sunday rather than lying in for the cosier 9 o'clock or the positively luxurious 11. Nuns from time to time would drink sour milk in front of their pupils in classrooms, to show that keeping body and soul together need not descend to a wretched taste sensation. Rough cloth was plainly more acceptable material to God than anything kind to the skin. (This one turned in very handy in the 40s, when Christians were drafted into the army, and forced in defence of the right to wear something made out of sandpaper.)

It is pleasant to be able to report of Thérèse of Lisieux that she was against heavy corporal penances. This is surprising in its way, because she was a Carmelite nun, and Carmelites of her time had written into their rule a rigid observance of Church fasts, and little details like taking the discipline three times a week. Thérèse, as a conformist bourgeois, rarely went against received opinion, but at the Carmel of Lisieux she made an exception. A certain Mere Marie de Gonzague was novice mistress when she joined, and her contribution to the general gaiety was to advise her novices to roll in nettles when no better penance was on offer. Held up for the community's admiration was also one Blessed Henry Suso, a thirteenth century Dominican who had carved the initials IHS over his heart, spilling quite a bit of gore in the process, and used to sleep on a door studded with nails. Thérèse thought all this over, and wrote in *L'Histoire*:

'... I've heard so much about saintly people who took on the most rigorous mortifications from childhood upwards, but I've never tried to imitate them – the idea never had any attractions for me. I expect that comes from cowardice on my part... I could easily have devised a hundred minor ways of making myself uncomfortable. Instead of that, I've allowed people to wrap me in cotton wool, to treat me as a bird that's being fattened for the market, as if there were no need for penance in my life at all...'

She considered she had lived a 'good life' at home, adored by her well to do father, spoiled as the youngest of the family by her sisters, her existence darkened only by the fact that her mother had died when she was barely five, leaving her for years after prone to tears at the drop of a hat. She had not entered a cloister to bring that essentially comfortable life with her, but on the other hand she saw no reason to thrust it high-mindedly away from her as a worthless and self-pampering past, either.

Thérèse was in fact a new sort of nun. The intemperate Jansenist nineteenth century in France was drawing to its close, casting up on the shores of penitential exhaustion its gaunt refugees. Thérèse thought the interior dispositions of the religious, and in particular the degree of simplicity she was able to bring to the dedicated life, more important than slavish obedience to traditional monastic practices. The Blessed Benvenuta Bojani, who had bound her lower body so tightly with an iron chain that eventually she had to have surgery to get it off, would have despaired of her.

But for all her common sense in this regard (and we would put it at no more than that these days), Thérèse could be bit of a crepehanger when she wanted to be too. She wrote once, pondering *joie de vivre* generally:

'... sometimes I felt very lonely, just as I did when I was at school... Feeling depressed and ill, I'd often repeat to myself a line of poetry which brought peace and strength back into my soul: it runs "Time's but a ship that bears thee, not thy home". Those words cheered me up when I was quite small, and even now, when so many of my childhood's impressions have disappeared with the passage of the years, this image of the ship appeals to me, and helps me to bear this life...'

Against the 'cheered me up', one somehow wants to insert (*sic*). But it is clear that as a saint and exemplar to others (though to be fair to her, she never had any plans in that direction), Thérèse suffered from an odd disadvantage. Though she was cheerful and considerate to others and duly deferential to her Maker for the miracle of creation, she had no talent for human happiness.

There are such people. They are detached from human life, and are often deeply confused about it, in extreme cases declining into hypocondriacs or depressives. Nothing like that was true of Thérèse. But as a mere babe she would creep away for long periods to a private place behind the bed, not so much seeking solitude, which even small children can sometimes crave, as to be separated from her companions and *alentours*. She thought the earth basically ugly and the heavens beautiful, and she had a kind of contempt for certain wealthy friends who 'served God... at the same time enjoying to the full the good things of earth'. She later wrote that God was teaching her the art of mental prayer by thus alienating her from everyday living, but like old Rodriguez, one cannot help wondering a little about the true motivation.

Then later, as a schoolchild, Thérèse would not participate in games. While the others romped around in the playground and delighted in their physical existence, she would go off on her own and lean against a tree, 'indulging in graver thoughts'. After a little she took to burying the birds that dropped from the tree (there seem to have been a lot of them, for some unexplained reason), and made of her little graveyard a melancholy corner of the

Abbey schoolyard. Here she was joined by a handful of other little girls, both puzzled and somehow drawn by her abstraction, to whom she then used to tell stories that she made up as she went along. The stories appear to have been cheerful enough, and she certainly had a talent for telling them that she relished exercising. But it was a pale diversion.

Throughout *L'Histoire*, you get the impression that she is forcing herself to enjoy as much of existence as she possibly can. God is ineffably good for simply not having made it all rather less pleasant than it is (which he would seem to have had a perfect right to do). Group activities, whether dancing quadrilles with cousins (boring) or doing embroidery with the Children of Mary (worse than useless), palled, and human conversation was 'cloying... even when about holy things'. People in the mass seemed (an evocative phrase, coined once when she was ill) like no more than 'a great string of onions'.

In 1887, when Thérèse was 14, Louis Martin took her and her sister Céline on a pilgrimage to Rome. The voyage was meant in part to divert Thérèse from a recently conceived obsession with becoming a Carmelite. This was quite barmy, the kind of fixation that young girls can sometimes get on an ancient institution or an older man. Thérèse proposed to enter the Order when she turned 15, which was manifestly impossible, because the Superior of the Carmel of Lisieux (the Cure of St Jacques, the technical or 'ecclesiastical' head) had decreed that she could not be received before she was 21.

Thérèse undoubtedly enjoyed the 'worldly' side of her venture into the bright blue yonder. She came out of her shell from the first day on, and surprised everyone (perhaps even herself) by chatting happily with pilgrims of all ages.

Passing through Switzerland, she wished passionately that she could be on both sides of the railway compartment at once, since distant snow-capped mountains soared into the skies in one direction, commanding open-mouthed attention, whilst in the other a fairy-tale village clung to an escarpment, its church tower canopied by shimmering white cloud. Regarding the night heavens over the Alps and thinking of her future – she would come out of her shell with a vengeance in Rome and make a bold representation about entering Carmel to the Pope – she wrote later:

'... when the testing time comes, I shall be shut up within the four walls of Carmel, and my outlook will be restricted to a small corner of this starry sky. Very well then, I shall be able to remember the sights I'm looking at now, and that will give me courage. I shall find it easier to forget my own unimportant concerns as I contemplate, in my mind's eye, the greatness and power of the God whom I try to love above all things...'

She was beginning unexpectedly to rejoice in the earthly world, and quickly reminding herself of how she really felt. Temptation can wear curious masks. Reason, which is to say melancholy, returned to her throne in the Campo Santo cemetery in Milan. She was 'delighted' (it is the word she uses) with the tombs and monuments when she and Céline wandered pensively among them:

'... you felt you wanted to offer them your sympathy, these men and women of stone, so life-like were they, so calm and resigned in the expression of grief. That child over there, throwing flowers on the grave of its parents... you would swear that the wind was scattering them as they fell, just as it seems to blow back, here a widow's veil, there the ribbons that bind the hair of a young girl...'

For Venice, she actually uses the term 'melancholy'. The city confirmed her *mal du siecle*. 'Even the palace of the Doges,' she writes dismally, 'its huge rooms with their treasures of gold and carved wood and marble, with their masterpieces of painting... so many years now, since those vaulted rooms echoed with the sentence of life or death passed by those stern rulers! When we went round these horrible places of confinement (the cells), it carried me back to the days of the martyrs: and I would gladly have stayed there for a bit to see what it was like...'

Martyrs and a preoccupation with their lot overwhelmed her in Rome, naturally enough. She had always felt a powerful attraction to the heroes of the early Church, and claims to have 'dreamed' of shedding her blood as they did. In the Colosseum, the sheer romanticism of it suddenly got the better of her. She and Céline found they were prevented from going down into the actual arena where the martyrs had died by a barrier. Abruptly, at a cry from Thérèse, they hitched up their skirts and leapt over the obstacle, skittering down the piled-up masonry to the level where chariots had once pounded and lions roared. Despite shouts from the guides – and indeed Louis, who found this behaviour from his little daughters disconcerting – they got to the circus proper, and fell to their knees to kiss the dust. Thérèse records that her heart was thumping fit to burst. Either she got a prodigious kick out of breaking the rules, or she could only come truly to life in proximity to death.

The contrary thing is that basic common sense seems to be what has endeared Thérèse to the people who have been moved to admire her. *L'Histoire* is to the present day read by as many hard-heads as hysterics, and commended as a practical text, laudably suspicious of anything too far out, on guard against fakes and phoneys. Yet there were attitudes Thérèse espoused, values she cherished, even modes of expression she countenanced, that she must have known could not but alienate a large number of her readers. (The rejoinder to that is of course that she did not know she was going to have any readers, her writings were simply an act of obedience towards her superiors.) Yet there remain the rather more disturbing reflections which she indulged shortly after her First Communion, when she could have been no more than nine years old:

> '... I felt a great desire for suffering spring up in my heart, together with the conviction that our Lord had a lot of crosses in store for me... Suffering was now the magnet which drew me to itself: it had a charm which thrilled me, although I had never experienced it...'

Against 'charm', one again yearns to insert (*sic*). The 'charm of suffering' is not something which commends itself to many paid-up members of the human race. Coming from a nine-year-old, even one early schooled in spiritual lore, it is distinctly troubling. But Thérèse expressed herself in this way on more than one occasion, and suffering was to remain a 'magnet' for her all her life: so that what she meant in the context must be appreciated if one is to get near to an understanding of her.

Many will share the young woman's natural melancholy, and to some her death wish will not seem entirely alien. What is called 'the divine discontent' is a not uncommon condition, even among the less than saintly. But for a mere girl to cry out for pain and anguish as a 'gift' seems so disconcerting that we are reluctant to view her merely as one shy of pursuing pleasure any more, or as unadapted to human happiness. She goes on a breath (a small shudder?) later:

'Oh yes, I had suffered, but without any love of suffering: it was only then (after First Communion) that I was conscious of a real attraction for it... I found myself repeating those words from the *Imitation*: "Jesus, sweet to the taste beyond all telling, turn all earthly consolations into bitterness for me". That prayer came quite naturally from my lips, without any effort on my part: I felt as if I were repeating it automatically, like a child repeating a formula heard on the lips of some grown-up person she's fond of...'

It is interesting that she writes here of a child repeating a formula. Her mother Zelie before she died had certainly imbued her daughters with the notion of always conforming themselves to the will of God (which was nineteenth century shorthand for grinning and bearing it). She may have been in a general way preparing them for the sacrificial life of the convent. Zelie had wanted to be a nun herself, and let her girls know how bitterly disappointed she had been when she was rejected by the Sisters of Charity. By coincidence, Louis too had tried religious life (at the Great St Bernard monastery), but he had failed because he had no Latin. Both saw their 'deprivation' as a cross to bear. Then Louis once on a visit to the church of his childhood had found himself (most contrarily) 'too happy' in his life with his family, and had prayed inspirationally 'to suffer something for Thee'. The child Thérèse, one would like to think, learned her collect a little too well. There is after all little consistency in objecting to Henry Suso and the door spiked with nails, if you simply mean to wish on yourself a painful cancer, a crippling sickness or a violent wounding.

But then it was the nineteenth century, when people rolled in nettles rather more routinely than they do now. Anaesthetics had been introduced in hospitals, but they were still fairly primitive, and not yet wholeheartedly blessed by the Churches. When Queen Victoria used chloroform to assist in the birth of one of her children, a Spurgeon-like preacher (obviously not anticipating a knighthood) railed against those who 'robbed God of the cries of women in labour'. The more moderate religious settled for a simple if-you-can't-beat-'em-join-'em attitude. It is too easy to go on about sado-maso-chism, whether in convents or public schools. Severe pain was pretty well inescapable in the world as the Victorians knew it, and since it was a bit of a dream to think you would ever be able to cancel it out, a way had to be found of dealing with it. Stoicism was a proud, pagan remedy, suited only to proud, pagan souls. So 'embracing suffering in union with Jesus on the cross' became a standard therapy.

Thérèse, in as much as she thought about it at all, would certainly have accepted that suffering on earth could neither be eliminated nor alleviated much. She would not have been hugely interested in advances in medical science (yet she would not have been contemptuous of them, either: she saw 'God's hand' in the progress of mankind). They merely had nothing to do with the case. To the age-old poser 'Why does a merciful God permit suffering?' she would have been inclined to retort 'Why not?', since it seemed to her that suffering was in its mysterious way the result of the very human evil that had done down Jesus. (There is a truth lurking deep in this: certainly the worst suffering in human life has ever been the entirely avoidable hurt inflicted by one's fellows.)

But for all that, Thérèse would have appreciated that Jesus, blameless Son of God, need not have submitted himself to suffering. Others abided the question, he was free. The Redemption may require the Incarnation (God becoming man), but it does not strictly demand the Passion or the Crucifixion. In other words, for mankind to be redeemed, it is quite sufficient that the son of God should become a human being. Nothing further is required. The historical Jesus thus might have lived out a peaceful and pedestrian human life, teaching and selecting people to continue his work, in the fullness of time being 'taken up' to his Father without physical suffering or death. There was no necessity for Calvary.

But Jesus, Thérèse saw clearly, had chosen suffering. This could only be because he had embraced humanity without conditions, and as a consequence needed to share the lot of humankind to the full. It appeared evident to her that she must make the same election. She neutralised any dilemma arising by deciding to become a 'victim of love'. Now this was not in the event one of her saccharine evasions.

The idea had matured in her as she brooded on certain religious of her time who offered themselves as 'victims to the divine justice', believing they could thus turn aside and bring on their own heads the punishments merited by sinners. It was a concept of spiritual substitution confidently described as 'heroism'. Thérèse pondered:

'I felt this self-immolation wasn't at all the one I wanted to make. The cry of my heart was something different: "My God, why should only your justice claim victims: why should there be no victims of your merciful love?" Everywhere that Love is misunderstood and thrust on one side: the hearts on which you are ready to lavish it turn away towards creatures instead... If your justice, which finds its scope on earth, demands to take its course, how much stronger must be the impetus which impels your merciful love to take possession of souls! Your mercy, we are told, reaches up to heaven itself. Jesus, grant me the happiness of being such a victim, burnt up in the fire of your divine love!'

To be a victim of love might at least be easier on the sensibilities (not to say the nerve endings) than being a victim of justice. There is not the same 'go ahead, take a swing' element. The position is the rather more reasonable one of Jesus before his Father. The very devout often choose to forget that the Son of God invoked a get-out clause in his hour of trial.

Father, everything is possible for you. Take this cup away from me. But let it be as you, not I would have it... Being a victim of justice anyway was a plain nonsense, given even half-way sensible understanding about God:

> 'I feel confident that the fire of love can sanctify us more surely than those fires of expiation: why should our Lord want us to suffer unnecessary pain? No, there's nothing that can bring us comfort like this way of love: for me, nothing matters except trying to do God's will with utter resignation...'

Thérèse was a wide-eyed child at the foot of the cross, observing love as she had not seen it before. She wondered what the formula was, so that she might obediently repeat it.

In a certain sense this understanding closed her mind and heart to any pursuit of pleasure as the rest of us might comprehend and acknowledge it. There she stood on Calvary in her First Communion dress (Marie had made it for her with loving care, Zelie having been sadly prevented from doing so), the white veil beneath the crown of roses spattered with the indifference of the world, bright diamonds of tears gleaming in her helpless eyes. She would never move from this spot. She would never relinquish the clarity of vision accorded to juvenile eyes. She would never grow up.

It was an engagement she was totally true to.

Today apotheosised as a saint in glory, she remains the Peter Pan of the heavenly choir.

Her 'Way of Childhood', for which she became posthumously famous, was no more than a theological reflection of her own prolonged immaturity. The notion is one of utter dependence on God. It is the precise contrary of the do-it-yourself philosophy of the masochist-penitents. They flogged themselves half to death because they had to show how desperately earnest they were about holiness. Thérèse believed in leaving all that to somebody who knew more about it.

She recommended the helpless dependence of a child on its parent. Kids don't know how to prove a point. Isolated in childish understandings, Thérèse presented herself to the God who does not betray or slam kitchen doors in your face as a poor bewildered orphan. She never used the image 'God the Mother', but that was because she did not possess the insight of a Julian of Norwich, and anyway all through her spiritual development remained an unrepentant bourgeois. But she thought it somewhere beneath the surface. Her whole doctrine is a cry for a maternal cuddle, and the highest thing she can say about her earthly father is that his unselfish love for his children after Zelie's death made him as 'good as a mother'.

The vision of the world throughout *L'Histoire* is resolutely ingenuous. Thérèse behaved like a helpless (and even incompetent) child well into her young nun-hood. She developed a little-girl habit of meeting every difficulty in religious life with a ready smile (less chance of upsetting the grown-ups if you beam prettily), and she used regularly to drop off to sleep in choir in the early mornings, so that the other nuns at Lisieux would gently shake their heads and tolerate this pleasant, dim little creature, who had somehow or other bluffed her way into their enclosure (she had succeeded in getting in at 15, after all, despite considerable opposition), and might even make a proper Carmelite one of these days, you never knew.

Once, when she was ill as a child and her sisters were worried about her health (never totally robust), Thérèse observed dreamily: 'Let God play the part of Papa, he knows what is best for baby.' Marie demanded a little sharply, 'Are you a baby, Thérèse?' 'Oh yes,' replied Thérèse seriously, 'but a very wise baby. A baby who is an old man...'

In Shirley Temple terms, it was a cute angle. Only the truly unsophisticated can hope to negotiate it and win. It was a question of getting the priorities right. Jesus had given her the cue when he got tired of his disciples arguing about who was going to be top dog among them, and had called a little child to him, thrusting the puzzled girl or boy into their midst, proclaiming: *Unless you change and become like little children you will never enter the kingdom of heaven.*

So there, would have muttered babyish, wise Thérèse. The meaning is clear even to the most untrained mind. To me the interior dispositions are what matter, and those of a child, naturally loving, trustful, without guile, unreasoning, are the only ones to opt for.

Unripeness was ever her defining note. She simply rejoiced in her child's eye on a sadly grown-up world. When she thought of the moments in her life that had most gladdened her, they appeared naturally to be those of infancy. Herein lay her only concept of pleasure, her only notion of what was worth pursuing for personal gratification. She recalled with delight draughts round the family table – songs with her sisters – a child's watch given to her by papa – the thrill of being called pretty by adults, or complimented on her silky hair by grown women concerned about theirs.

And thus her abnegations and penances had also to be small, childish, as it were family things too: putting up with the harsh word from another – bending to a companion's need – not objecting when somebody splashed you doing the washing – suppressing one's own desires and keeping one's little sufferings quiet in case they burdened an associate. These 'little' things were as close as a half-pint like Thérèse could get to the mega-penances of the old Fathers of the Desert. But they were superior, she thought a touch rebelliously, because they proceeded from a more reliable source.

And that source was love. It was love that enveloped the helpless child, and thus only love that could lead the 'little' soul to anywhere near that goal of all religious, the perfection of God himself. 'Our

Lord's love makes itself seen quite as much in the simplest of souls as in the most highly gifted,' she wrote joyously, 'as long as there is no resistance offered to his grace. After all, the whole point of love is making yourself small: and if we were all like the great Doctors who have shed lustre on the Church by their brilliant teaching, there wouldn't be much condescension on God's part, would there, about coming into hearts like these?

'But no, he has created little children, who have no idea what's going on, and can only express themselves through helpless crying: he has made the poor savages, with nothing better than natural law to live by: and he is content to forget his dignity and come into their hearts too – these wild flowers that delight him by their simplicity...'

It was a comprehensive theology. It wrapped up ecclesiology, soteriology, the missionary problem and everything else. Little children just trust their parent. Their business is not to work things out or fret over problems, but just to take things as they come. They need to stay little. Safe and protected. Only thus will they be informed of what is healthful and noxious in the garden about them, in what they should delight and find pleasure, in their beautiful, corrupted, vitiated, wonderful adventure playground of a world.

2.

Thérèse
and Love

I was glad to leave Bologna, wrote Thérèse a little primly in the account of her pilgrimage to Rome in 1887. 'It was utterly spoilt for me by the University students who crowded its streets and hedged us in wherever we went on foot – especially by a brief encounter I had with one of them.'

She was 14, and the cryptic entry hardly bespeaks a solidarity with her own generation. The 'brief encounter' which so put her off, however, remains a little mysterious. It seems she was trying to get down off the train as her party arrived in the city, and a student suddenly appeared from nowhere, gave a hoot of delight and grabbed her, whirling her bodily around, and depositing her none too gently on the platform. He was probably an industrious lad, who later became a notable doctor or advocate, and cared for his old mother, but seeing this pretty girl uncertainly descending the steep steps from the carriage, thought he would be failing in both gallantry and youthful resource not to go to her aid.

In Hollywood films, such trivial incidents commonly lead to eternal romance. But Thérèse did not like the script at all. It is arguable that it was one of the rare occasions that a male other than her father or an uncle or cousin had touched her. She was most precise about her chastity (already firmly decided upon: Zelie's nudging towards religious life again), and may even have refrained from games at school because it would mean possible physical contact with little boys. There are none so rigid as the inviolate young. But the experience on Bologna station obviously troubled her, for she passes over it rather too quickly in *L'Histoire*, and hurries on to an edifying if thoroughly dull visit to Loreto and the Holy House.

The starchy reaction at least proves that she was normal. She was suddenly, literally breathtakingly, swept into an area of human experience of which she knew nothing, but which she believed herself to have forsworn. Even so, it could turn the mind botheringly from a chosen bloodless aim. Did Carmel suddenly wobble and fade ever so slightly before a student's cheeky grin?

A pall or radiance (according as you care to view it) of chastity hung over the Martin household. As has been said, all five of the girls entered convents, and there never seems to have been a time when they were not thinking of religion. A worldly career presumably was not an option, and marriage had a curiously low profile *chez Martin*. The parents had done all the marrying that was strictly necessary, so there was no need to go on about all that.

Nobody is on record as keeping company, and there would not even seem to have been young male friends. Even allowing for the stricter social and sexual mores of nineteenth century bourgeois France, this is remarkable. Thérèse writes of childhood parties, at which little boys must have been present, and one strains to hear the giggle of hanky-panky behind the gooseberry bushes. But it never occurs. It may be that mother Zelie, having from the beginning instilled crystalline principles into her daughters, successfully inhibited them, or that Thérèse – a bourgeois to the fingertips that guided her pen – carefully edited out anything that might 'scandalise'. But she writes movingly and intensely about the love of God, so as with her namesake the 'great' St Teresa, there would seem to have been identifiable passion beneath the starch.

To judge from her writings, sex for Thérèse was apprehended simply as an accident of nature. Love for its part came under three formalities. First there was family love, and this she vaunted and praised to the skies. 'God has seen fit to surround me with love at every moment of my life,' she wrote, 'all my earliest impressions are of smiles and endearments. And if he planted love all about me, he planted it in my childish heart too, gave me a loving and sensitive nature. How fond I was of Papa and

Mamma! I shewed my affection for them in any number of ways...'

Indeed, she worshipped her parents. Zelie was 'the best of mothers', and together with Louis eventually became elevated to 'the blessed stock from which we all sprang'. On the pilgrimage to Rome, there was 'no finer figure of a man in the company than Papa'. An adoring daughter, she invests Louis' modest person with a charism that outshone that of all the bishops, priests and important citizens who comprised the rest of the party.

Her elder sisters were stars in her heaven. She had a crush on Pauline. It was announced early that Pauline was 'certain' to be a nun, and the infant Thérèse immediately declared that she would be a nun too, without having the slightest idea what it could mean. But Céline, her immediate senior, also quickly became more than just someone to share a house with. Thérèse would leave her dessert unfinished on the table to go off with Céline when the other got down, and when Céline's four years' seniority meant that she must begin lessons (with Marie, the eldest: school came only after basic instruction at home), Thérèse went along too, sitting quiet as a mouse in a corner through whatever was going on, simply to be near her sister.

It was all desperately cosy, the very crochet stitch of *L'Histoire*. But such family affection was par for the course (not to say a condition of domestic peace) in days when women's lives were circumscribed by the four walls of their homes. Yet ripples could occur on the tranquil sea. Léonie, 10 when Thérèse was born, ran into big trouble with Zelie. The girl was constantly ill, unable to get on with other children and seemingly mentally backward, so that mother and daughter grated on each other. There were ugly confrontations. Thérèse chose not to face them, for she makes no mention of the least trouble in paradise. (We learn of the difficulties with Léonie from Zelie's letters.) Nothing must cloud the serene sky of family love.

Then there was the love of friends. Thérèse had certain difficulties about this. It was something for which, in the same way as with personal happiness, she proved to have little talent. She esteemed friendship, even sought it quite earnestly at one point, but it always somehow evaded her. The few children who came to the house at Lisieux never amounted to much more than neighbours to whom one was being polite, or casual acquaintances. When she went to the Abbey school, however, there were two girls that she came to like a lot. She does not say what in particular attracted her to them, but obviously the youngsters could talk together, swap ideas and whisper secrets, so that the foundations of lasting friendship were being laid. Then one little girl had to stay at home for a while. When she came back, the outcome was a bit unexpected:

'... how carefully I kept the little ring she'd given me! And I was delighted when she came back. But I found, to my chagrin, that I only got cold

41

looks in return. Well, there was no appreciation there, and I wasn't prepared to go about asking for affection when there was no disposition to give it. All the same, God has given me a constant nature: when I love with a pure intention, I go on loving, and I still pray for my old school-fellow, she is my friend still...'

Thérèse says nothing of the second little girl, so presumably something of the same sort happened there. She seems to have been puzzled by her failure to make friends, indeed baffled. She offers the distinctly censorious judgement: 'I was fond of them both, and they were fond of me too, in as far as they were capable of it: but the love bestowed on us by our fellow-creatures is so limited, so fickle!' In any event, it was a question of once bitten twice shy. She knew herself to be possessed of a sensitive, affectionate nature, and if she could not find someone to appreciate the depth of her feelings, she would not expose herself to unnecessary hurt. She would sooner give friendship up as a bad job.

Mind you, she appreciated this was a bit perverse ('pride', in nineteenth century spirituality-speak), and in the event began to worry about herself. 'I had no knack of winning other peoples' good graces,' she laments. Yet Céline did not suffer from the same disadvantage, and that seems to have bothered Thérèse further. Céline at length formed a 'special friendship' with one of the mistresses, which drove Thérèse to something like envy. 'I would have been glad to follow her example', she understates decorously, teeth grinding ever so gently in the background. A pretty and warm little girl, whose only repellent habit as far as her schoolmates were concerned would have been always to know her Catechism backwards, Thérèse was desolate at being without a 'best friend', and disregarded by teachers into the bargain.

She was a stubborn little person, however, and it could thus have been her quiet self-assertion which accounted for the loneliness and unpopularity. It lasted all her life, and she appreciated it was a fault in her. Whatever the reason however, with hindsight Thérèse decided to see her rejection during schooldays as a kind of blessing:

'Lucky for me that I had so little gift of making myself agreeable: it has preserved me from grave dangers. I shall always be grateful to our Lord for turning earthly friendships into bitterness for me, because, with a nature like mine, I could so easily have fallen into a snare and had my wings clipped: and then how should I have been able to "fly away and find rest"?

It is somehow typical of Thérèse, concerned as ever only with the 'small' things of life, to draw such a large reflection from a petty incident of childhood. There were of course times when people fussed over her and made her the centre of attention, and she did not with hindsight object to that. The sudden affection towards her seems to have been gratuitous. When you're in you're in, she might ruefully have reflected. She remembers for example the nuns at the retreat where her hair was so savagely brushed as in general 'taking more trouble about me than about any of the others'. It was a retreat leading up to First Holy Communion, and the headmistress would come round every night with her lantern, pausing to give Thérèse a special loving kiss as she lay in bed. The little girl found herself deeply touched by this. Kisses and kissing were an earnest of serious affection for her.

She was always kissing people. Zelie for a start, and then when Zelie died, her substitute-mother Pauline. When Pauline entered Carmel Thérèse at once fell ill, crying for 'Mamma' and her embraces. Marie came. Thérèse thus rose from her sick bed and started kissing her. It got to an osculatory peak when it was Marie's turn to go into the convent. Thérèse wails: 'I couldn't leave her alone for a moment, this dearly-loved sister who was so soon to take her flight. Goodness, how I must have tried her patience ! Every time I passed her door, I knocked till she opened it and smothered her with kisses as if I were laying up a store of them for all the years in which I should have to do without them...'

And then her First Communion is described as a kiss from Jesus: a 'lover's kiss'.

How much precisely Thérèse knew about sexual love is of course conjectural. From *L'Histoire* you can divine evidence of both a profound ignorance and a suppressed knowledge. It would certainly have been unusual for the daughters of the bourgeoisie of the period to be left totally in the dark about sex, because the middle-class world was full of Steerforths, and a Steerforth behind the bushes with a cloth-headed girl could result in that shame of shames, unmarried pregnancy. Most bourgeois fathers feared this more than debt. Indeed, it amounted to the same thing. The lower orders might kick the shame-less hussy out of the house, but if you occupied a position in society you had to bear the cost bravely, and send the stupid bint away to Provénce for a while. (Or England, if you really wanted to pay her out.)

But on the other hand, the infection of Jansenism* in the French Church meant that among Catholics, sex was something that was not really mentioned. Some things, it seemed, were better left unsaid. Jansenism was really just Calvinism under another name, so there was precisely the same tongue-tied diffidence about the divine arrangements for the propagation of the species. Girls from farms or country estates were probably better off than their city sisters, because they could see things happening in the fields which left no doubt in their minds as to the Creator's *idee-maitresse*. The rest just had to take their luck as the hay rolled.

Zelie, while clearly an ice maiden at heart, was not a chump. Thus the Martin girls would almost

* Catholic rigorism, named after Cornelius Otto Jansen, 1585-1638, bishop of Ghent.

45

surely have been educated in the mysteries of the flesh, and made aware of the perils consequent upon less than fastidious behaviour. As for sexual games, experimentation, they were all 'touching people', and would perhaps as children have assisted each other in the exploration of their bodies. But Louis and Zelie would both have policed all that pretty strictly. Thérèse was always demanding to sleep in the same bed as one or other of her sisters, but there was no indication it was for any other reason than that she was the baby of the family, and regarded it as her cosy privilege. She was, and remained, singularly innocent.

But a serpent moved beneath the floorboards of *Les Buissonnets* (the spacious house of the Martins). It was extraordinary, provoking sober reflections about gnats and camels. The matter concerned Zelie's *bête-noire*, Léonie. It may even have come about because Léonie was her mother's bete-noire. Details are scarce, but there appears to have been a servant in the household called Louise, who did not move as easily as the daughters through the pervading pall of chastity. She began to dominate Léonie, principally it would seem with the hope of subverting Zelie's authority in the house, but what precise means she employed to get the girl in her power is not clear.

Zelie was simply horrified when she found out about it – she was a sick woman by this time, soon to die of her cancer – and at once dismissed Louise, swearing she would live without servants thenceforward whatever it cost her. Things improved between her and Léonie from that point on. Whether Thérèse, the merest infant at the time, knew anything of the strange and unlikely business, we cannot tell.

Thérèse as a child never played with dolls, and had great confusion with genders in learning her native language. Something of her attitude to sexuality may be divined from this. The difficulty about genders could indeed signify a reluctance in her inner self to come to terms with 'the he and the she of it' (Joyce). While increasing in age and wisdom, she was not growing up in the usual sense of the word, and so could have opted to remain isolated in female nature. The all-female family had proved marvellously supportive. Louis was a lovable old dear who didn't interfere. Why change anything?

Then the failure to play with dolls could indicate a lack of interest in offspring which might seem unusual in a nineteenth century female child: and which in turn could point to a dislike/fear of genital activity. Not many middle-class Victorian woman relished anyway the notion of what they must undergo to bear children. Many saw it as a fate they had to embrace, or finish up the maiden aunt in the second storey back. Unless of course they were Catholic, and thus could become nuns.

'Why aren't there Jewish nuns ?' wails the switchboard girl in *Bells Are Ringing*, sick of men, sick of the world, sick of a woman's lot. It is a question worth pursuing in another context. Here it simply indicates that for a Catholic girl disenchanted with the idea of a husband and a sexual life, there was another outlet. An interest in nuns had begun for Thérèse with the murmurs about Pauline, and increased as Zelie shared her frustrations about religious life with her.

Then Louis used to take Thérèse for childhood walks to the chapel at the Lisieux Carmel, where he would point out the grille to her and whisper of the women who passed their lives behind it. Thérèse writes that the suspicion never crossed her mind that a mere ten years later (she would have been about five at the time of these walks) she would be behind the grille too: but a seed had unquestionably been sown, for she was clear from the outset that she wanted to be not just any old nun, but an enclosed Carmelite. This is a specialised and unusual vocation.

To be a nun, dedicated, removed from the world, essentially pure, answered questions that Thérèse was at this point only beginning to ask. It was not that she despised or ignored her sexuality. It was rather that she thought, once having seen the world *sub specie aeternitatis*, that her sexuality was one of the last things about her that mattered. It would not even last very long: only as long as a life which, even if it went on for 80 years, was still but a short prelude to the eternal, sexually neutral life to come.

In the 'kingdom', after all, we neither marry nor are given in marriage. The alternative seemed to be students sweeping her off her feet in Bologna: fun and even delightful in its way, but not a patch on the 'real thing'. Religious ecstasy was infinitely preferable to the hurly-burly of the *chaise longue*. You didn't have to upset the single blessedness of your life for it, and into the bargain you got to bed early. Primal urges could thus be profitably put on the back burner.

Thérèse had discussed her strategy and general approach to the problem with Our Lady of Victories in Notre Dame Cathedral on her way to Rome. She had a special devotion to Mary crushing snakes and other symbols of the male supremacy under her heel. Joan of Arc in her armour was all her life a favourite saint too. Thérèse recalls:

'... I asked Our Lady of Victories that she would keep me clear of anything that might tarnish the purity of my mind... I dreaded the encounter of evil things which were still a closed book to me: I had yet to be taught that nothing can be unclean for those who have clean hearts... I prayed to St Joseph with the same intention. I had a devotion towards him which was closely bound up with my love for our Lady: so I said, each day, the prayer which begins "St Joseph, father and guardian of virginity"...'

Virginity, purity of mind was not seen to come automatically, anyway. Innocent Thérèse was not so green as to believe the rebellious flesh could necessarily have no power over her. She saw things in her own nature that others may have been blind to. The Carmelites of Lisieux who wondered about their new, dim little member and how she would fit into the community would hardly have seen Thérèse as a Jezebel manqué, a Madame Bovary. But Thérèse did:

> '... it was only God's grace that preserved me from giving myself up to the love of creatures: without that, I might have fallen as low as St Mary Magdalene did. I find comfort in those words of our Lord to Simon the Pharisee: "He loves little who has little forgiven him"...'

The Lord was in the house of Simon the Pharisee when the penitent woman (who was only arguably Magdalene) burst in and washed his feet with her tears, drying them with her hair. Yet the absurdity of the comparison must have struck Thérèse even as she penned it. Curse my fatal innocence, she may have thought. How could she suppose she had the capacity to be an abandoned sinner when she wasn't even sure she had the ability to be a half-way saint? Her response to the flawed emphasis is important, because it is in a sense the heart of her 'Way of Childhood', in which, as you would suppose, imaginings can loom larger than facts:

> 'But I, you say, owed him little ? On the contrary, I owe him more than the Magdalene herself: he remitted my sins beforehand, as it were, by not letting me fall into them. Oh dear, I wish I could explain exactly what I feel about it. Put it like this – a clever doctor has a son who trips and falls

over a stone, and breaks a limb. His father is at his side in a moment, picks him up tenderly, and treats his injuries with all the skill he has...

'But now suppose the father sees the stone in his son's path, runs ahead of him and takes it out of the way, without calling any attention to what he is doing. At the time, the boy is unconscious of the danger he would have run but for his father's foresight... But if he learns afterwards what risks he has been spared, the boy will love him more than ever...

'And that's what God's loving providence has done for me... He hasn't waited to make me love him much, like the Magdalene: he's made me realise what I owe to his tender foresight, to make me love him to distraction, as I do. When I'm told that an innocent soul can't love as much as a repentant soul does, how I long to give that sentiment the lie!'

Her First Communion had been a 'lover's kiss' from Jesus, and now behind the grille of Carmel, she loves her lover 'to distraction'.

Thérèse writes exactly like an impressionable girl of a later era who never misses a Friday night at the pictures. Modern nuns too must shiver a bit as they read this sort of thing, for the sexual imagery does not occur much in religious life these days, any more than the enveloping (contrarily, sex-affirming) clothing. It was probably only ever there because it was thought a woman could not be defined ex-

51

cept in terms of relationship with a man. *Love is of man's life a world, a thing apart. 'Tis woman's whole existence...* (Cowper). But Thérèse for her part happily refers to Jesus as her 'spouse', and characterises herself as that shriek-worthy *metisse*, a 'bride of Christ'.

This latter *mal pensée* is so developed as to make the devout of today draw a sharp breath. About a week after she formally took the veil, Thérèse's cousin Jeanne got married. Thérèse describes how she at once wrote to this young woman, anxious to learn what were the little attentions a new bride lavishes on her husband. She thought her attitude towards Jesus should not be less studied (it is her word again) than that of Jeanne towards the man she had admitted to her chamber. There is something mildly endearing about it, perhaps. But then, a moment later, she blows it. 'I amused myself,' Thérèse writes, 'by sketching out a wedding invitation of my own, modelled on hers: and this is the way it ran...' (The document is here quoted in full, to give the full and faintly horrendous quality.)

'Letter of invitation to the wedding of Sister Thérèse of the Child Jesus and of the Holy Face.

'Almighty God, Creator of heaven and earth, Lord of the whole world, and the glorious Virgin Mary, queen of the heavenly court, invite you to take part in the wedding of their Son, Jesus Christ, King of Kings and Lord of Lords to Thérèse Martin, now invested by right of dowry with two freedoms, those of the Sacred Infancy and of the Passion, her title of nobility being derived from the Child Jesus and the Holy Face.

'Monsieur Louis Martin, the Heir-in-Chief of all Misfortune and Humiliation, and Madame Martin, Lady-in-waiting at the Court of Heaven, invite you to take part in the wedding of their daughter Thérèse to Jesus the Word of God, Second Person of the Blessed Trinity, now by the operation of the Holy Spirit made Man, and Son of Mary, the Queen of heaven.

'Since it was impossible to invite you to the ceremony of the nuptial blessing, to which only the Court of Heaven was admitted, on 8 September 1890, you are asked to be present at their return from the marriage tour, which will take place tomorrow, that is, the day of eternal reckoning, when Jesus Christ, Son of God, will come on the clouds of heaven in the splendour of his majesty to judge the living and the dead.

'The hour of this being still uncertain, you are asked to hold yourself in readiness and be on the watch.'

There is of course an element of wit in it. It could be blasphemously funny in the hands of the Monty Python team. But it is impossible to think that Thérèse intended anything satirical. She had a sense of the ridiculous which could bubble up in unplanned jests during recreation with her sister nuns, but these were all of a childish nature. It was not in her character to make a joke about things that she regarded as holy, or elements in her life that defined her. The bourgeois conscience would have baulked at that. (The reference to Louis as 'Heir-in-Chief of all Misfortune and Humiliation', incidentally, is a strangely infelicitous allusion to the fact that her father had by now suffered his mental breakdown and was in an institution, with only Céline still outside a convent to care for him.)

The 'wedding invitation' can only be seen as a grave *jeu d'esprit*, an effusion of the little girl who never grew up, and as a consequence didn't quite understand the boundaries of taste. Thérèse found herself both intrigued and embarrassed when faced with the behaviour of the adult world, and probably thought she sounded grown-up by simply trying to echo it as faithfully as she could.

Amor divinis, which is the third formality under which Thérèse apprehended love, fortunately does not require its devotees to be mature. The little child lisping prayers at the bedside, saying thank you God for the Tracker bar and auntie Sandra not coming to tea like she was supposed to after all, loves God more certainly than the dogged saint and scholar, desperately trying to avoid distractions and concentrate on his/her devotions. The trick in fact is to try and preserve (or re-discover) that essential naivety. It is not easy, and few succeed. Thérèse could not fail.

And as far as love itself was concerned, Thérèse was quite convinced. The 'science of loving' lay solely in unconcern. Detachment was the key. She was fond of quoting the *Book of Proverbs*, where Wisdom is represented as proclaiming from the city's heights 'Who is ignorant? Let him step this way' ('Simple hearts, draw near me' in the old translation of Proverbs 9, 4, which may be closer to Thérèse's thought), and from Isaiah 66, where the prophet has God proclaiming 'I will console you like a mother caressing her son: you shall be like children at the breast, fondled on a mother's lap'.

'Oh dear,' cries this young Doctor of the Church, lost for the *mot juste*, 'when God makes promises like this, what's left for us except to keep silence before him with tears of gratitude and love? If all the weak, imperfect souls in the world could only feel about it as I do – I, who am really the least considerable of them all – there'd be no reason why a single one of them should despair of scaling the hill of charity and reaching the very top. Our Lord doesn't ask for great achievements, only for self-surrender and gratitude...'

(She then rubs it in, since it is to be a major tenet of her soteriology.) 'It isn't that he wants us to do this or that, he just wants us to love him...'

She felt it was her duty to shout this from the housetops. Or, hidden away in Carmel and vowed to silence, to embroider it on an anti-macassar (granted her needlework turned out good enough). There was so little she was any use for except loving.

And there was so much to be taught about love. She thought of Magdalene again, Magdalene with her tears and flowing hair, Magdalene the supposedly fallen woman, guilty of loving unwisely but not of failing to love, as the exemplar of the trust she burned to instil in all human hearts:

'... that boldness of hers, which would be so amazing if it weren't the boldness of a lover, won the heart of Jesus, and how it fascinates mine ! I'm certain of this – that if my conscience were burdened with all the sins it's possible to commit, I would still go and throw myself into our Lord's arms, my heart all broken up with contrition: I know what tenderness he has for any prodigal child that comes back to him. No, it's not just because God, in his undeserved mercy, has kept my soul clear of mortal sin, that I fly to him on the wings of confidence and love...'

Thérèse was desperately ill when she wrote those words. It was early July, 1897, and she was already only able to use a pencil to set them on paper. They mark the end of her manuscript. The pencil fell from her hand as she wrote that final word. 'Love'. It was the last word she had to say to the world.

3.

Thérèse

and the

Job in Hand

In the mid-thirties, in my hometown of Auckland, New Zealand, a Carmelite convent was founded in the suburb of Mount Eden. A large bungalow set in woodland was converted, and a weatherboard chapel built. Nuns were brought from Australia to inaugurate the foundation, released from their enclosure for the transitional period.

When the canonical barriers came down again, however, the Wars of Religion broke out. New Zealand was still very largely a WASP* society, and a correspondence worthy of Augsburg erupted in the newspapers. Devout and good Protestants could

---

* White Anglo-Saxon Protestant.

perhaps understand nuns who taught in schools or nursed the sick, but nuns who simply boxed themselves in and only spoke to the rest of the world through a curtained grille were surely Rome at its most reversionary. All that sort of thing was supposed to have stopped with Henry VIII. Why were they locking themselves in like that? Or were they locking us out? What were they for?

It has always been a problem explaining (even to observant Catholics) the precise purpose of contemplative nuns. There seems to be not the same difficulty when it is contemplative monks, for the overtone there is not 'shutting up beautiful young women in ugly convents'. Even if you detail the nuns' means of survival – which will generally involve subsistence horticulture and modestly remunerative 'holy' tasks, like the making of altar breads or church vestments – it says nothing at all about their *raison d'être*.

When Pauline Martin first got her idea about entering a convent – which Thérèse of Lisieux at once echoed – it was about joining the Visitation sisters. Now the Visitation sisters (Thérèse's aunt was one) were not an enclosed order. As their name implies, they were more concerned with works of mercy than recondite religious endeavours. The Carmel of Lisieux even 'spooked' the Martin girls a little for a start. Thérèse was taken into the chapel on their walks often enough by Louis, but it is stretching the truth to pretend that she was immediately attracted to the life of the sisters. In fact a couple of mortuary urns sculpted on the convent's gate positively put her off. (The nuns had not put them there, oddly enough: they dated from a previous occupancy, when the wealthy owners had displayed a *memento mori* to show that their minds were on higher things than the deceits of gracious living.)

The Lisieux Carmel had been founded from Poitiers, inaugurated by two professed nuns from that city, and four eager young postulants, two of whom as it happened were blood-sisters, and had put up their modest fortune to purchase the old house. The foundation was placed under the protection of a slightly dotty Prince of Hohenlohe, who was celebrated in religious circles as a thaumaturg, and had somehow or other got himself consecrated titular Bishop of Sardica (wherever that may be).*

Carmel is a very ancient religious Order, brought to Europe from the Holy Land by St Simon Stock in the thirteenth century, but reputedly dating back to Old Testament times. Its many houses down the centuries have been sanctuaries of contemplative prayer, and the Order boasts among its great members St Teresa of Avila (a reformer who in fact saved Carmel from sliding off the religious map), and St John of the Cross, the theologian and poet.

One day however the *Visitande*-elect, Pauline, went into the church of St Jacques in Lisieux (whose

---

* Bishops without a diocese are consecrated for an ancient one, these days a deserted geographical postage stamp.

cure was the ecclesiastical superior of the Carmel in the Rue de Livarot), and kneeling before the statue of our Lady, suddenly got the idea that her vocation might be to prayer rather than action. A young aspirant had died on the eve of her entry to Carmel, and it seemed Pauline could take her place if she wished. She did. The whole thing happened rather quickly, and must have been a bewilderment to Thérèse. But then she too had an inner revelation. (It ran in the family: Zelie before her death had practically depended on 'illuminations' in tight spots.) The words in which Thérèse expresses her particular change of mind are important. She writes: 'I felt that Carmel was the desert where God wished me to hide myself.'

The key concepts are 'desert' and 'hide'. The inclination to creep away from the haunts of men and give yourself in secrecy and silence to prayer, which this phrase perfectly expresses, is badly understood in the modern world. The East retains a tradition of reclusive 'holy men', but in the West anchorites and contemplatives (*a fortiori* hermits) are thought at best eccentric, at worst obscurantist. Prayer in the age of organised welfare and computer technology can represent little more than the sad survival of wishful thinking. Those who would truly help the world go out and lay water pipes in drought stricken areas or found bush hospitals. They do not pause to ponder, as Hopkins did, that *the Holy Ghost over the spent/World broods, with warm breast and with/Ah, bright wings.*

Yet it was not just funny old Christian mystical gropings and Pauline's lead that drove Thérèse into the Carmel of Lisieux. There was also the sobering knowledge that deep down, face it squarely and stop messing, she was not much good for anything else except praying.

Thérèse had always had the opposite of an inflated idea of her own abilities. It was based on a shrewd and realistic assessment of what she was and where she was going. She knew herself to be not in any sense a skilled person. She had done well enough at school perhaps, even occasionally coming top in things like history and essay writing, but they were things she liked, and anyway it does not seem the standards were very high. Her uncle, Isidore Guerin, harder-headed – for property reasons he was the legal guardian of Louis' daughters until they came of age – quite frankly thought her a dunce. She notes this without embarrassment. She even amplifies on it sunnily:

'... well-behaved and good-natured, to be sure, and sound in my principles, but clumsy and incompetent. It wasn't surprising if that was the impression my uncle and aunt had, and no doubt still have: I was too shy to talk much, and when I put anything down on paper, my horrible scrawl and my spelling, which can only be described as original, didn't make it very attractive...

'When I did bits of sewing and embroidery, the result was all right and satisfied the nuns, but the awkward, ungainly way in which I held my work justified the low opinion people had of me... I got accustomed to hearing a lot about other peoples' intelligence and nothing about my own, so I concluded that I hadn't got any and did my best to get on without it...'

Today we would say that she was robbed of self-esteem, and thus had no choice but to conceive of herself as second rate. But the rubbishing at least caused Thérèse to reject lines of endeavour at which she might have proved no more than half-way good. An earnest little soul, she would have broken her heart, diligently reaching for the moon. Yet prayer was attractive to her, and came naturally, and did not seem to require any special abilities. And in her understanding of reality, prayer achieved quite as much as work. In fact a sight more.

At one point during her nine years in Carmel, it was announced that a daughter-convent was to be opened in Indo-China. Thérèse responded enthusi-astically to this project, having always dreamed of being a 'missionary'. But her health was an obstacle. Disappointed, she reflected that anyway she would again be no good at trekking through jungles or mastering unfamiliar tongues in which to proclaim the gospel – she simply had not, and would never have, skills of that sort – so what missionary work she was capable of would have to be done in Lisieux rather than Saigon. That was perfectly possible, given the doctrines of the Mystical Body and the Communion of Saints. She gave her little girl shrug, flexed her knees, and went back to her *pre-dieu*.

Yet though prayer came naturally to her, it does not mean she prayed easily. There is an apparent contradiction here, but it is by no means unusual. The gift of prayer is akin to the gift of art. A composer or a painter wants desperately to do what s/he alone can do: but for all that the art is seldom produced effortlessly. We all know the old bromide about 10 per cent inspiration and 90 per cent perspiration. Well, the monks of old had a motto, *laborare est orare*. This is generally translated to mean 'work is prayer': but Latin being the delphic tongue it is, it can also be construed to read 'prayer is work'. As any mature monk after the long stint of matins and lauds would tell you, you pay your money and you take your pick. Prayer can indeed be a task.

Thérèse put on her working clothes, rolled up her sleeves and got down to her gift. The major difficulty for her was 'distractions'. Her mind tended to rattle off like a child's toy train on another line whenever she wanted to concentrate. The distractions got so bad that she came to think of them as a special penance which had been visited on her: an ironic cross to bear.

Then, just to make it easier, her prayer companions began to get on her nerves. There was a nun who always sat behind her and sucked her teeth, and another who rattled her rosary beads. This sort of thing, as is well known, can lead to murder in a silent cloister. In addition, she disliked the entire business of 'prescribed' devotions. Even the Divine Office became an obstacle for her to surmount. She preferred praying in her own way. She reflects:

'... I can't face the strain of hunting about in books for splendid prayers – it makes my head spin. There are such a lot of them, each more splendid than the last: how am I to recite them all, or choose between them?... It's a terrible thing to admit, but saying the rosary takes it out of me more than any hair shirt would: I do it so badly! Try as I will to put force on myself, I can't meditate on the mysteries of the rosary: I just can't fix my mind on them...'

Yet prayer, she had decided, was her calling in life. It was why she had entered Carmel. It was what she was for. So what was she to do? How to handle it right, this one thing she felt truly confident about? The little girl beneath the grown-up scapular again came to her aid:

'I just do what children do before they've learned to read: I tell God what I want quite simply, without any splendid turns of phrase, and somehow he always manages to understand me... For me, prayer means launching out of the heart towards God: it means lifting up one's eyes, quite simply, to heaven, a cry of grateful love from the crest of joy or the trough of despair: it's a vast, supernatural force which opens out my heart and binds me close to Jesus...'

The vast, supernatural force was in fact a detailed, mundane chore that just happened to transform reality. This was its purpose, as indeed it had to be hers behind the grille. Those who prayed were the energy of those who did the practical, sensible things. You should 'do' nothing about which you had not prayed, she had learned from the spiritual masters. But there was no time for prayer out in the busy world. So a dedicated group, a special cadre, had to do it. The saints, the 'great friends of God' knew the scene backwards:

'... St John of the Cross and St Thomas and St Francis and St Dominic all went to prayer to find the secret of their wisdom: a divine wisdom which has left the greatest minds in admiration. "Give me a lever and a fulcrum," said the man of science, "and I'll shift the world." Archimedes wasn't talking to God, so his request wasn't granted: and in any case he was only thinking of the material world. But the saints really have enjoyed the privileges he asked for: the fulcrum God told them to use was himself, nothing less than himself, and the lever was prayer. Only it must be the kind of prayer that sets the heart all on fire with love: that's how the saints shift the world in our own day, and that's how they'll do it to the end of time...'

Yet the prayer that sets the heart all on fire with love didn't just happen: you had to be conscientious, workmanlike about it. When Thérèse was ordered by Pauline to write her autobiography, she first wanted to know how on earth she would find the time to set her thoughts down on paper. Her day, she complained, was completely taken up with 'earning her living'. It was her artless estimation of what she did. She went to the chapel each morning as the farmer to his field. The ploughing and planting had to be done if the harvest was ever to be reaped. She even regarded idling (i.e., not getting on with the praying) as a breach of her vow of poverty. The lot of the poor was constant toil. The lot of the Carmelite was continual intercession.

It was the starch in her soul again, perhaps. But she felt it necessary to be as earnest as this, because she was aware of an anomaly in religious life that might not apply down on the farm: it was terribly easy to 'goof off' – to swing the lead and do everything by means of a hypocritical pretence. Nobody would ever know the difference.

Again there is an analogy with art. It is hard to insist that the gifted actor, say, must always perform at his peak: yet many a major performer has been criticised for under-employing his talent. You should make good use of a gratuitous gift. Similarly, Thérèse saw, a contemplative nun is free to do as little or as much for God as she pleases. God will let not fly thunderbolts if she lies back and relaxes. There will not even be a mild reproof from her Guardian Angel.

Much of Thérèse's 'Little Way' is to be found in this understanding. The service of God is essentially the service of a loving father. It cannot be anything else. And the loving father neither compels his children, nor rejects them when they fail. One has only to think of the prodigal son, and what he got away with, to understand the degree of latitude available.

Thérèse all her life claimed to have a great love of the Psalms that make up the bulk of the Church's official daily prayer, but she must have had to gloss over or mentally edit out certain parts of them. The God she loved and served was light years away from Jehovah fulminating on high. Thérèse the trusting infant could not conceivably have loved a God who showed himself to be less compassionate than she was.

In any event, the upshot of her attitude to prayer was that she saw that she must be a saint. This was a surprisingly cold, as it were professional, decision. She admits herself at one point that it sounds wonderfully conceited. But the 'daring ambition' struck her as proceeding out of an inescapable logic. If prayer was her work in life, then she was obliged to do that work as well as possible. But only a saint can pray really well. *Ergo*.

Of course, you do not become a saint merely by taking thought. It is not like deciding to be a plumber or an accountant. God must take the initiative. Thérèse was thus quick to add that she did not rely on her own merits, which she regarded as non-existent, but put all her faith in 'him who is virtue, who is holiness itself'. She recalls an incident from childhood which puts the matter in perspective for her:

'... a day came when Léonie, thinking she was too old now to play with dolls, came along to us (Thérèse and sister Céline) with a basket full of dresses and pretty little bits of stuff for making others... "Here you are, darlings," she said, "choose which of these you'd like, they're all for you." Céline put her hand in and brought out a little ball of silken braid which had taken her fancy. I thought for a moment, and then said, as I held out my hand: "I choose the whole lot!" Then, without further ceremony, I took over the whole basket...

'Only a childish trait, perhaps, but in a sense it's been the key to my whole life. Later on, when the idea of religious perfection came within my horizon, I realised there was no reaching sanctity unless you were prepared to suffer a great deal, to be always on the look out for something higher still, and to forget yourself...

'And then, as in babyhood, I found myself crying out: "My God, I choose the whole lot. No point in becoming a saint by halves. I'm not afraid of suffering for your sake: the only thing I'm afraid of is clinging to my own will. Take it, I want the whole lot, everything whatsoever that is your will for me."...'

A saint is not necessarily called upon to do great

things. That is just as well. If splendid achievement were a condition of sanctity, then Thérèse would have been down in the cellar with no takers. A saint, as has been noted by many a spiritual guru, is called upon to do ordinary things extraordinarily well. And ordinary things were what Thérèse positively waded in. Her day to day existence was so pedestrian as to make a call from the fishmonger seem an exciting event. In the entire calendar of saints, it is not possible to find another *beata* whose life was so circumscribed by non-events.

She rose at the crack of dawn to go to the chapel and pray. She ceased praying some hours later to take a meagre breakfast, and then divided her day between the work of the community and more prayer. She got landed with the washing often as not: a wretchedly monotonous scrubbing and beating out of resistant coarse cloth on stones. There were two periods of recreation during the day, after the main meal at noon and after supper in the evenings, when conversation was allowed. Otherwise a rule of strict silence applied. The nuns never went out, and it was long before a time when holidays away from the dear old patch were thought of necessary to psychological equilibrium.

Thérèse therefore saw that the 'ordinary' thing she could try to do extraordinarily well was keep the plodding rule. She disciplined herself heroically to obey it in its most minute particulars. There was a prescription that when the bell rang to call you to another task, you were supposed to leave whatever you were doing at once to proceed to the new work. If Thérèse thus found herself writing, shall we say, she would leave a letter half-formed rather than disobey this petty injunction. If any of this had been done in a sullen or resentful manner, it would have represented a pride for which old Rodriguez would have handed out infernal stars. But Thérèse forced herself to do it joyfully (which is not the same thing as patiently) to show her detachment, her willingness to serve, her appreciation of the insignificance of her own ambitions as against God's will for her.

She obeyed her superiors in the same spirit. 'Subjugating one's will to the will of another' had probably never struck Thérèse as a very easy or even sensible thing to do. It was supposed however to be the mark of the good nun, but none knew better than the ingenuous 'little white flower' that some fearful old bats could get control of the barn from time to time. Zelie had once described her last child as 'clever and obstinate', and so in the midst of a genuine desire to please, Thérèse indeed was. It was probably in fact what saved her in an ambience that could have sucked her in and digested her like so much porridge. Thérèse liked to do things 'under obedience' because in a roundabout way it preserved her independence of spirit. (You had to do what they said, you weren't choosing.) This may in fact be the very reason why Pauline, who knew her well, 'ordered' her to write her autobiography.

Thérèse to some extent always spoke with forked

tongue about her literary endeavours. She maintained they were no good, and that it was absurd to think anybody would ever want to read them. For all that, however, she enjoyed writing, and, it would seem, thought well enough of her own poetry. (It is in fact of variable quality, religious verse rooted in family life: much better in French than in translation.) But Pauline may shrewdly have judged that without the goad of a direct command, Thérèse's writing about her childhood might either not have emerged at all, or would have declined to self-indulgent twaddle. Her 'twee' style could so easily have become a parody of itself. (The irony here is that many a professional writer would probably be grateful – in retrospect – for a vow of obedience to force him to produce his manuscript. Sean O'Casey all his life kept on his study wall a single terse message to himself: GET ON WITH THE BLOODY PLAY.)

Thérèse began to understand (or may perhaps subconsciously have understood from the beginning) that her autobiography was an important composition. It is true she kept up her dispraise of it, and even gave Pauline permission to alter the finished manuscript in any way she thought fit. Exhausted and near death, she wrote:

> 'I have not had time to write what I wished to write. It isn't complete... Anything you want to cut or add to the notebook of my life, it is as though I were myself cutting or adding. Remember this later and have no scruples on the subject...'

But then, just a week or so later, the grim reaper so close at length she could hear the swish of his blade, she seemed to panic a little at her own judgement (or lack of it), and added, in terms which for Thérèse were remarkably stern:

'After my death you must not speak about my manuscript till it has been published: only to the Reverend Mother should it be mentioned (Marie de Gonzague again). Otherwise the Devil will set traps for you so that he may spoil God's work... such an important work...'

It is another characteristic of saints who achieve perfection through the long hard slog of doing ordinary things extraordinarily well that, for all their continued protestations of unworthiness, they are in the ultimate analysis not much interested in modesty. St Francis of Assisi, returning to his native city on one occasion, was greeted by a cheering crowd who set him on a donkey and lauded him through the streets, dangerously as though he were Jesus entering Jerusalem on the first Palm Sunday. The easily-scandalised Br Leo was appalled by this, but Francis, who saw in the greeting a recognition of God's work rather than anything relating to him personally, wondered rather if the reception had not been a touch restrained. Couldn't they have shouted their joy in the Lord a bit louder than that?

Similarly Thérèse, right at the end of her life, pushed out under the chestnut trees in the ancient rolling chair that had become her only means of mobility, breathed to the novice who was caring for her 'You know that you are looking after a little saint, don't you...?' No time for messing, no point in further dissimulation: she was God's work, just like the spiritual classic God had astonishingly dragged out of her, and anyone who couldn't see that ought to be told.

Thérèse's 'Little Way' of sanctity has received grave attention from serious theologians. It is acknowledged as a new departure, which for the first time brought the dizzy heights of holiness down to the level of ordinary people. Yet it is not unique. There have been plenty of spiritual teachers down the years to point out that the surest way to God is through humility and dependence. But what they failed to do was work out the ground rules, because (being scholars, divines, ladies bountiful or bluestockings) they lived that significant bit above the earth that everyday folk trod.

It is strange that there are very few gasmen or shopgirls recognised as saints by the Christian churches. (There are also singularly few married people, but that is a separate and rather darker question.) Numbers of dark-skinned martyrs have been ecclesiastically honoured, but possibly the only negro to make it as a 'confessor' is the ex-slave Martin de Porres. It is as though the calendar of saints were meant to be some kind of celestial Almanac de Gotha or Who's Who. Thérèse's spirituality rejects all that. She may be a bourgeois, but she is belligerently of the people.

The battles between good and evil which she fought, the spiritual victories she thus exemplifies, are desperately ordinary things: confrontations of the scullery or the workbench. The wild temptations of St Antony in the desert or the mocking of St Sebastian by his persecutors may represent the noble trials of heroic souls, but Thérèse is more concerned about the poor little souls, legion in number, who simply have to put up with people sucking their teeth at them, or klutzes at the next tub splashing them while they do the washing.

Thérèse saw the trivial trials of life as offering a martyrdom, and the only martyrdom available to ordinary people. The quick descent of the axe is in some ways easier to bear than that never-ending slurp in your left ear: that dreaded and regularly provided eyeful of soapy water. We will come to the maniac of the tubs in Thérèse's life later, but as regards the teeth-sucker (and this fault in fact was only one of a thousand things about the nun in question that got under the petals of the little white flower), Thérèse developed a technique, and bravely put it into practice:

'... I determined to treat this sister as if she were the person I loved best in the world. Every time I met her, I used to pray for her, offering to God all her virtues and merits... But I didn't confine myself to saying a lot of prayers for her, this sister who made life such a tug-of-war for me: I tried to do her every good turn I possibly could. When I

74

felt tempted to put her down with an unkind retort, I would put on my best smile instead, and try to change the subject...

'She was quite unconscious of what I really felt about her, and never realised why I behaved as I did: to this day, she is persuaded that her personality somehow attracts me. Once at recreation she actually said, beaming all over, something like this: "I wish you would tell me, Sister Thérèse of the Child Jesus, what it is about me that gets on the right side of you? You've always got a smile for me whenever I see you."...'

That, in Thérèse's book, was a victory comparable to St Lawrence's making cavalier jokes while on the gridiron. ('Turn me over – I'm done on this side.') It wasn't just a question of her getting along somehow with a person she found difficult, it was a question of her positively learning to love that person, because Jesus was 'hidden in the depths of her soul', and loved her as much (you believed) as he loved you. The defects of another might not be defects at all, seen in the right perspective. If God made creatures who can belch, then it is arguable that God meant them to belch from time to time, and not dismiss the function as an embarrassment, as tends to happen in polite society.

But the real genius of the 'Little Way' is that while it calls for heroic efforts in small things, it does not call for small heroes. Little children are very seldom courageous, and if the automatic reaction is to yell for mama in a crisis, well, there you are, that's kids. You can always live to fight another day. Or perhaps even learn to live with your cowardice.

Thérèse writes eloquently of her own faintheartedness. Once in the petty round of life at the Lisieux convent, she found herself falsely accused of dropping a heavy bunch of keys and waking a sick sister, as well as so startling a group of nuns that they almost took flight. Great were the recriminations:

'... I was the villain of the piece, and the poor sister I'd fallen foul of began to indulge in a long diatribe, of which the burden was: "That was Sister Thérèse of the Child Jesus making that noise! Oh dear, how difficult she is!" My story was quite different, and I wanted badly to stick up for myself, but fortunately a bright idea came to me – if I started to defend myself, could I hope to preserve my peace of mind? At the same time, I didn't think I'd enough patience to stand by and hold my tongue while I was being attacked like this: I'd only one chance left, and that was to run away...

'I quitted the field without beat of drum, leaving the sister to go on with her speech, which was reminiscent of Camilla's curse against Rome. My heart was beating so fast that I couldn't go any distance, I just sat down on the stairs to be alone with the spoils of my victory. It wasn't very heroic, was it? But I have a strong feeling that it's best not to engage in a battle when defeat is quite certain...'

Of such details, of such trivia, is human life made, and thus out of such details, such trivia is human sanctity achieved. Thérèse's mastering of her work in life, her vocation, her job in hand, demonstrates to the world at large that to be a saint is within the scope of all. The entrants in the Almanac de Gotha have lost any natural advantage they may have thought they possessed. Anybody can try for the everlasting crown.

You only have to be prepared to conquer yourself as much as you can, and to love – or at least to want to love, for the Little Way teaches you that genuine loving is not actually so killingly easy. Then you leave the whole thing up to the powers beyond you. It is their business more than yours, and in fact you do better not to interfere.

Your *cultus* may never be celebrated in your old parish or neighbourhood, and you may never be spoken of after you have gone as that glowing spirit who once supernally brightened our dull old suburb. But you will at least have a halo: as surely as little white flowers push through the grass every spring and rejuvenate a tired world.

4.

Thérèse
and the
Social Dimension

Social conscience has gone up in the world in our day.

It used to be individual morality that was supposed to compel you, but now you may plan and carry out a bank raid, say, and it will be argued that you are only taking from those who already have too much. (He who robs a bank commits a lesser crime than he who opens one – Brecht *passim*.) In the sexual area you can do pretty well as you please short of rape and murder, and expect to receive the approving comment of the newspapers (plus flattering pictures on the TV), and the envious support of liberals who would settle for just half your luck.

But try opposing a high-spending welfare scheme

in government, or promoting a tax haven, or lighting a cigarette at a Stockhausen concert, and see how far you get. The difference is of course that you are attempting to deprive/exclude/endanger fellow members of society, and that is the mortal sin. It sometimes seems that to jeopardise the rights or privileges of others is the only mortal sin left.

It has of course been famously said in recent times that 'society' does not exist. What there is, is simply an arbitrary collection of variously-motivated individuals. At the end of the nineteenth century this would not have been found an outlandish definition. The emerging Left was beginning to mutter things about the 'proletariat' and the 'capitalist oligarchy', but such abstractions were probably not comprehended in either the clubs of the gentry or the pubs of the working class. An individual enjoyed or endured the state of life to which he had been called, and that was that. (She too, but one social problem at a time.)

Louis Martin, Thérèse's father, had what we might recognise today as a social conscience, though it was religiously rather than sociologically inspired. He loved others in charity, and genuinely tried to be just in his dealings. High on the list of sins crying to heaven for vengeance in the old catechism was 'depriving the labourer of his just wage', and Louis, who employed men in his business and kept servants at home, was always punctilious about their treatment. He even fell into the habit of paying his bills the same day as he received them, so that he would not be unjust in business dealings. His creditors must have thought him estimable, but pious beyond the dreams of good book-keeping.

The noises coming from Rome on social matters were confusing, however. It was a period in which the Enlightenment was beginning to penetrate even to the murky recesses of the Holy Office, and loyal Catholics like the head of the Martin family found themselves pulled in a couple of directions at once. First there had been Pius IX's *Syllabus of Errors* in 1864, with its sweeping condemnation of 'liberalism', especially as manifested in developments like free speech, the separation of Church and State, religious toleration (one God, one point of view, was the Roman wisdom), and modernism generally. Then there had been the First Vatican Council, which the Franco-Prussian war had broken up before it could duly qualify its swingeing definition of papal infallibility with that of the infallibility of the Church. Now it seemed Leo XIII was rumbling about a 'family wage', and upholding the right of workers (to the alarm of many Catholic employers) to form trade unions.

Louis took refuge in the St Vincent de Paul Society. He was not on the available evidence much of a political animal, and thus probably did not bother his head too much with social theorising. But by banding together with his fellow bourgeois Catholics in the group founded by Frederic Ozanam, he was at least able to do something immediate and practical about the poor and needy on his doorstep.

The Vincent de Paul Society operated by setting up 'conferences' in local areas, the members of which would seek out those in material need, and then take them food and clothing (more rarely money) on formal visitations. Thérèse and her sisters thus sometimes went with their father on these charitable expeditions, and Thérèse in this way gained a first-hand if superficial knowledge of poverty. The tramps meantime who came to the door of the family home begging bread, or stopped the affluent-looking for a few sous in the street – and Louis and Zelie were always exceptionally kindly towards these – taught her a bit more.

But it was all at careful remove. The female children of the nineteenth century bourgeoisie were judiciously shielded from poverty. It was not so much a scandal as a disease to be caught. The relief of human misery was a man's business if it was anybody's: gently nurtured girls should not have to look upon the hovels of the destitute, nor have their nostrils offended by the smell of unwashed bodies. Respectable women could thus grow up only vaguely aware of another world out there, whose denizens constituted a separate and in their way alien species. The daughter of a wealthy Scottish family at the turn of the century recalled being assured by her grandmother when there was an accident, and a screaming farm girl lay trapped under their carriage wheels: 'Don't fret yourself, my dear, they don't feel pain as we do.'

Thérèse was sufficiently alive to the world as it

really was to acknowledge that she had led a remarkably sheltered life as a child. Even later, under the strictures of Carmel, she was able to write:

> 'Mother (she is addressing Pauline), look at the life I live here! Untouched by the anxieties which make the world such a miserable place – all I've got to do is carry out the work you've given me to do, such pleasant, such easy work! And then, all this motherly care you shower on me! I never feel the pinch of poverty, I've always got everything I want. But above all, here at Carmel I have your love and the love of all the sisters, and it means so much to me...'

Against 'I've always got everything I want', another (*sic*) needs to be sidled in: in fairness, Thérèse's needs were extremely modest, and the provision of Carmel for its adherents was far from lavish. They ate no meat, and barley soup and black bread was about as adventurous as the menus got. But none the less there must have been many a daughter of the poor who would have found herself happy to finish up in a nineteenth century convent. (Religious orders of the period took in 'lay sisters' from the proletariat, but otherwise recruited their members from the middle or upper classes: the curse of 'gentility' weighed heavy on female institutions until quite recent times.) Taking the three vows of religion at least put paid to that blank and not unjustified dread of the very poor: nothing whatever on the table come suppertime.

All Thérèse really knew about the poor was that she should love them, as Jesus had loved them before her. She was thus sentimental about those less fortunate than herself, and sometimes unwittingly patronising. 'Had I been free to manage my own property,' she once wrote magnanimously when she was a nun with a vow of poverty, 'I should certainly have been ruined, for I could never have borne to see anyone in need without at once giving him everything he needed.'

Today that would be called failing to solve the problem by throwing money at it. But she had first felt herself called to the active life, so in her heart and in her own way she had embraced an 'option for the poor'. She would not have accepted that by choosing to devote herself to prayer she was thereby ignoring or deserting the deprived and needy. Indeed she probably believed that intercession could even in some mysterious way ease hunger pangs. It was her analysis, and that of many other devout and not unconcerned Christians. God was in charge. What she could not do, someone else would be inspired to. As long as she prayed.

Thérèse's human sympathies were universal. The apostolate of prayer that she believed in encircled the earth. Carmelites were supposed to pray especially 'for priests' – it was a kind of political correctness in a clergy-ruled church – but that did not require or imply that the poor, the sick, the lonely, the dying, the despairing, should be relegated to second place. They were all out there suffering somewhere, and the exchange rate for prayer and sacrifice was quite high enough to guarantee plenty to go round. Otherwise the doctrine of the Mystical Body was pious claptrap, and people like Carmelites might just as well pack up and go and live an easy life on the Riviera.

Thérèse even conceived a strange sympathy with neighbours in God who 'lose their souls'. Now this in the context was odd pastoral theology. The saving of souls was as it were the 'end product' for contemplative nuns: you interceded for peoples' material welfare, their health, the success of their crops, all so that they could have sufficient freedom from care to turn to God and thus enter his kingdom. But it was Christian teaching that you could, through your own fault, exclude yourself from the everlasting realm. It was mysterious and distressing. Thérèse consequently writes:

'I'm always ready to sympathise with the people who lose their souls – after all, it's so easy, once you begin to stray along the primrose path of worldliness. To be sure, once your soul has been raised up, even in a small degree, above the common level, you see bitterness in all the pleasures the world has to offer, and the longings of your heart are too large to be contented with ephemeral praise. But if God hadn't called me from the first, if the world had lavished its smiles on me all along, what mightn't have happened to me...?'

The odd theology lies in the fact that 'those who lose their souls' would be in the understandings of the time enemies of God, thus abandoned to Hell and impossible to love or feel any sympathy for. Thérèse's blithe unorthodoxy ignores this lecture hall severity. She goes further, reaching out to the demons themselves, Satan's minions, who in Dantesque imagery stoke up the 'real fire' that chastises yet does not consume the damned. This relates to a childhood dream, and she records it all with childish solemnity:

'One night (I dreamt) I went out for a walk alone in the garden, and when I got to the bottom of the steps that led up to it, I stopped, overcome with fright. In front of me, quite close to the tunnel one has to go through, there was a barrel of lime: and on it I saw two horrible little demons, dancing about with a surprising quickness of movement – surprising because they wore flat irons on their feet.

'All of a sudden their flashing eyes fell on me, and thereupon, apparently much more frightened of me than I was of them, they jumped down off the barrel and took refuge in the linen-room, just in front of them. Their nervousness encouraged me to go and see what they were up to, so I went up to the linen-room window: there they were, the poor little demons, running about over the tables in a frantic effort to get out of sight. Sometimes they would come up to the window, looking anxiously to see if I was still there: and finding that I went on watching them, they began to run to and fro as if in desperation...'

Thérèse interpreted this dream to mean that the soul, when in a state of grace, has nothing to fear from the spirits of evil. But that is far too po-faced. What she imagined in sleep is a pure Disney cartoon, with Snow White/Thérèse discovering to her wonder and delight an empathy with all living creatures, even the wicked and ugly ones who have strayed out of the Wild Wood. (If somebody were only to love them, would the little dears still behave like that?)

Thérèse's universal compassion was best exemplified in the case of Pranzini. Now Pranzini was a notorious murderer who was going to die on the guillotine. Thérèse was still a schoolgirl when all this occurred, 14 or so and highly impressionable. Louis would not permit his girls to see the newspapers (fearing they could be damaged by them: how would he have been a father in the TV age?), but he spoke about the case at the dinner table, for in 1887 the name of Pranzini was on every lip. Thérèse reacted with concern and motivated disquiet to this tale of –

' – an abandoned wretch who'd been condemned to death for his appalling crimes, and there was every reason to think that he would die impenitent. He must be saved from Hell! I tried everything: there was nothing I could do myself, but I could offer to God our Lord's infinite merits, and all the treasury of his Church: and I would get Céline to have a Mass said for me – I didn't like to ask for it for myself, because I was shy about owning up it was for Pranzini, the wretched man I'm speaking of...'

The 'wretched man' did not see himself in this negative light. He was a defiant crook, with a modest standing in the criminal community, and thus a position to keep up in jail. He wanted to die with due dignity, spitting in the eye of his guards. Born in Alexandria, Pranzini had murdered two women and a girl of 11 whilst robbing a safe in the Rue Montaigu in Paris. He demonstrated no remorse during his trial, and after his condemnation filled in the time before his execution translating pornography: extraordinarily, he was something of a linguist, and could pick up a bit of money rendering into French texts that a discreet readership was ready to pay well for. Why he wanted to go on earning a living when there would soon be no life to spend it on is not clear, but some compulsions die hard.

He retained however a superstitious devotion to the Virgin Mary. There was no saying where this came from or why it persisted in him, but Thérèse was delighted when she found out. She regarded it as a trump card in her hand. She turned to the Blessed Mother and any saints whom she imagined would exert themselves, praying fervently.

'... Céline didn't make fun of me,' she rushes on, caught up in her soul-saving enthusiasm, 'on the contrary, she wanted to give me her help in converting my sinner (as she called him). I was only too thankful: I would have liked all of creation to join with me in praying for the grace that was needed...'

A thoroughgoing campaign was under way. All resources were being diverted to the fight. It is of course curious that Thérèse makes no mention of Pranzini's victims at any time. Nowhere in her account in *L'Histoire* does she pause to shed a tear for them. One can speak of bourgeois complacency too easily: but the directness of purpose, the concentration on a solitary aim to the exclusion of all else, would have done credit to an entrepreneur out of the stockbroker belt. Thérèse is absolutely determined to save Pranzini's soul:

'... by way of encouragement in this practice of praying for sinners, I did ask for a sign. I told God I was sure he meant to pardon the unfortunate Pranzini, and I'd such confidence in our Lord's infinite mercy that I would cling to my belief even if Pranzini didn't go to confession, didn't make any gesture of repentance. Only I would like him to show some sign of repentance, just for my own satisfaction...'

Thérèse demonstrates why the middle classes

will probably always win. She can be smug and dependent at the same time. The reason perhaps that she thought less of 'her' sinner's victims than she might have done was that she thought of them as already in God's hands, and after all, that was the place to be when all is said and done. It was for people still in this world that you put on the prayer-pressure. They seemed curiously unaware of God's hands. And for his part, unless he was firmly told about it, and the troops called in to convey the message as powerfully as possible, God at times honestly seemed unaware himself that certain people were in dire need.

Thérèse got her sign. The Pranzini campaign paid off in spades. 'My prayer was answered, and to the letter,' she reports, over the moon, full of joy, faith, tearful gratitude. 'Papa didn't allow us to read the newspapers, but I thought there could be no harm in following up the story of Pranzini. The day after his execution I came upon a copy of *La Croix*. I lost no time in opening it, and what I read brought tears to my eyes, so that I had to hurry away and conceal my emotion.

'Pranzini didn't go to confession: he went up on to the scaffold, and was just preparing to put his head between the bars of the guillotine, when a sudden inspiration came to him. He availed himself of the crucifix which the priest was holding out to him, and kissed, three times, the sacred wounds. And with that his soul went to receive its award, from those merciful lips which told us that "there will be more rejoicing in heaven over one sinner who repents, than over ninety-nine souls that are justified, and have no need of repentance"...'

It was a bourgeois triumph. Grace works on nature, the spiritual doctors tell us, it does not change it. Somebody other than Thérèse, a daughter of the poor say, would perhaps have prayed just as earnestly for Pranzini, but would have been paralysed with shock, wide-eyed and trembling, when it transpired that a prayer by the likes of her had actually been heard. But the Little White Flower, without inhibition, in whose mouth butter wouldn't melt, was able to take it in her stride. *Bien sur.* Papa always comes through with the necessary when you convince him just how badly it is needed. He takes perhaps a little more wheedling these days than he used to. But once he sees how much his Little Princess really loves him...

Yet her bourgeois nature could occasionally do Thérèse a disservice too. She did not look back with any pride on the day she lost her temper rather unnecessarily, and kicked a servant girl.

It was a storm in a holy water stoup, but a great failure of charity. Improbably enough it was something to do with the religious celebrations known as May Devotions. And Thérèse was soberly aware she would not have behaved in such a way to one of her sisters, or to a social equal. Unable to go to church with the family one childhood day, she had determined to have her own May Devotions, and thus set up little bits of candle and flowers before the statue of the Virgin. (May is traditionally the month of Mary, and the devotions are hymns and prayers in honour of the Blessed Mother.)

Victoire, a young maid who was looking after her, came in, and Thérèse piously asked her to begin on the *Memorare* while she lit the stubs. Victoire responded with a snort of laughter: there was enough of all that when Madame was around. Thérèse was inflamed. It was an insult to *la Sainte Vierge*. She shouted at the maid that she was a 'naughty girl' – and let fly at her with a hard kick.

Victoire was more surprised than hurt. Thérèse writes of the 'look of astonishment' that came over her face. But she knew her place. Uncomplaining, she reached into her pocket and produced some pieces of taper she had found in the kitchen and was in fact bringing in for the 'little girl's game'. Thérèse was at once humiliated and ashamed. She burst into tears.

It was not the only run-in she had with Victoire. Pride or class (or both) met head on a second time. (Did it indicate the growth of a new social awareness in Thérèse? Were the two fighting out in the domestic arena the precise social battle which Gambetta and President MacMahon were simultaneously waging in Paris?) Thérèse wanted an inkpot which was on the kitchen mantelpiece, and being too small to reach it, asked Victoire to fetch it down for her:

'... would she do it? No: she told me to get up on a chair. Well, I went and got the chair without saying any more about it: but it did seem to me it wasn't very nice of her, and by way of making that clear, I fished about in my childish vocabulary for the most offensive word I knew... Before I got down off the chair, I turned round with a dignified air and said: "Victoire, you're a brat". Then I ran for cover, leaving her to digest this deep insult...'

Victoire did not take this one lying down. As a daughter of the poor she was perfectly used to sticks and stones, but names she was not going to put up with. She hollered for Thérèse's elder sister Marie, who came running, and was taken aback to discover what her junior had said. There were ways in which one simply did not behave with servants. She made Thérèse apologise, which Thérèse duly did, but 'without being really sorry'. 'If Victoire wouldn't even stretch out her long arm to oblige me,' she sniffs, the pique still glowing years later, 'what else would you call her?'

Carmel, inside whose charitable walls such pettinesses amounted to a breach of rule, cleared what remained of bourgeois snobbery out of Thérèse's system. She never again thought of people as fixed in the condition of life to which God had called them. (Though she was no reformer: she arguably swallowed all the malarkey about the socialist beast at the gates proceeding from those Catholics who still thought of *Rerum Novarum* as evidence of an Antichrist in their midst.) She was too busy praying, and wondering if she was doing any good at all for society by her life of sometimes pointless-seeming invocation and sacrifice.

It is a particular affliction of saints that they come to be very unsure indeed about what they are doing and why they are doing it. John Mary Vianney, the Cure d'Ars, whose life was virtually a template of humble dedication, thought towards the end of his life that he was much too grasping and self-centred to have any chance even of being saved. Bonhoeffer in Flossenberg concentration camp came to look on his theological impulse and writings as a bitter waste of time, instead of which he should have attempted something useful in life. Thérèse was to die young, so her sense of futility came over her when she was barely 18 years old.

It was while she was in retreat for her profession as a Carmelite, which should have been a period of great peace and joy for her. But she began to suffer from critical doubts, which got progressively worse. Was there really any point in what she was doing? Could she ever be remotely sure that she would achieve anything at all for her brothers and sisters in God? At length, on the eve of the day when she was to take her vows, she made the Stations of the Cross, and there before the representations of the Passion...

'... my vocation seemed to me a mere dream, a mere illusion... Darkness everywhere: I could see nothing and think of nothing beyond this one fact, that I'd no vocation. I was in agony of mind: I even feared (so foolishly that I might have known it was a temptation of the devil's) that if I told my Novice Mistress about it she'd prevent me taking my vows...

But she got over that one. The darkness retreated with the dawn to make her profession day serene and unclouded – figuratively that is to say, for snow fell although it was only early September: and Thérèse, who was very fond of snow, contrarily saw this as a 'wedding gift from her bridegroom' – but it was a foretaste of things to come. The devil, or whatever agency was at work, resumed operations after only a brief pause, and doubts then remained more or less as a constant for the rest of Thérèse's life as a nun.

There were reasons for her misgivings. While she was an eternal child, Thérèse was essentially a wise child. She thus knew herself to be living a contrary life, dependent on faith alone for the confidence that her daily round of prayer, suffering and obedience mattered in the least. There was no way of demonstrating that her sacrifice, which had cost her dear – she missed her father desperately, and would be beside herself when he had to be committed – was remotely meaningful or would ever have a consequence for the world. You just had to accept that that was so. Believe it. Despite the appearances. Despite the devil mocking at you.

Céline, whose confidante Thérèse had been virtually all her life, both at home and in the convent, knew her mind-set. In the deposition she gave to the canonisation process years later, she explained how 'practically' her sister had thought of things. 'The religious life seemed to her,' she states, 'above all, a means of saving souls. She had even thought of becoming a missionary nun to this end: but the hope of saving more souls by mortification and self-sacrifice determined her to shut herself up in Carmel... She considered that it was harder to nature to work without ever seeing the fruit of one's labours, without encouragement, without any kind of diversion... And so it was this dying life, precious above all others for the salvation of souls, that she wanted to embrace, hoping, as she herself said, to be made a prisoner as soon as possible in order to give souls the joys of heaven...'

So walling up young and beautiful women could have a point after all, granted it was the young and beautiful women themselves who did the bricklaying. It was a life without much consolation, of course. Thérèse never sought spiritual joys, and was generally surprised and grateful if they came her way. She saw her true business as 'trading wholesale': immolating herself like Jesus, that was to say, so that through her identity with the Head she might reach the Members.

'Don't think of me as buoyed up on a tide of spiritual consolation,' she wrote in her letter to

Marie, the second part of *L'Histoire*. 'My only consolation is to have none on this side of the grave. As for the instruction I get, our Lord bestows that on me in some hidden way, without ever making his voice heard. I don't get it from books, because I can't follow what I read nowadays: only now and again, after a long interval of stupidity and dryness, a sentence I've read at the end of my prayer will stay with me: this for example: "You want a guide to dictate your actions to you? Then you must read in the book of life, which contains the whole science of loving"...'

It was a carefully chosen random quotation, for the words are those allegedly spoken by Jesus to Margaret Mary Alacoque, the seventeenth century visionary of Paray-le-Monial, who initiated the devotion to the Sacred Heart. This devotion has been so successfully guyed by those who set out to promote it – bleeding hearts crowned with thorns, surgical diagrams superimposed on pre-Raphaelite images – that the scoffers have been left without an icon to break. But it was intended initially as an expression of the humanity of Christ, which in its turn expressed the overwhelming love of God. Thérèse thought of Margaret Mary as definitely one of her circle. The 'science of loving', to be 'read in the book of life' had become her preoccupation too.

'Love,' she writes, 'is the vocation which includes all others: it's a universe of its own, comprising all time and space – it's eternal...' She meant that though doubts would always plague her, deep down there was no enduring problem. If you could love, you could accept anything. She knew she was no apostle, no martyr, no doctor, no saint of charity, but after all none of that really mattered. What mattered was being at one with God at work in his universe, meeting the regular beat of the pulsing heart. 'I'd found my vocation,' she writes a little deliriously, after having analysed Paul in Corinthians on the apportionment of gifts and on charity, 'and my vocation is love! I have discovered where it is I belong in the Church, the niche God has appointed for me. To be nothing else than love, deep down in the heart of Mother Church: that's to be everything at once...'

Hysteria, some will say, and nod wisely. Quietism, the social activists and those attracted to liberation theology might more moderately judge. But the fact it is that if you truly learn to love in this life, you do not any more balance the books as others do. True loving is not something easily entered up. You have done violence to original sin, and that will bring some rather original accounting in its wake. Most people manage only a pale reflection of love, something caught in a glass, darkly: those who contrive to love at the source are rare, dangerous, unsettled and unsettling individuals.

For most, loving at the source involves too many contradictions to be feasible. Dante could recognise the love 'which moves the sun and all the stars', but then back away from it, leaving it to Beatrice in glory (how and why she got there, none of his business) to try and out-dazzle the anomalies.

And if such love, love which reaches out to every man and woman, lies behind the appearances, what then is the meaning of the anti-love negatives? Of pain, suffering, and cruelty? 'Man's forgiveness give and take' cries old Omar Khayaam. The fact that he was too tight to allow that the same Creator he accused had also thoughtfully provided him with his jug of wine, his book of verse, and of course Thou, is not to be held against him. He speaks for a genuinely confused race.

Thérèse in her way attempts to answer that confusion. She notes somewhere in *L'Histoire* that before she learned to love, she used to want to change people 'for their own good'. In other words, her compulsion was to rush out and reform the world. One can picture her reincarnated in our own day (hopefully in rather better health), jetting out to Africa, racing around remote villages in her jeep, sinking wells, inoculating children, rounding on idle males and complacent females, getting it all done as it were in spite of the people she has come to help.

But this desire for dominant, purposeful involvement left Thérèse as she came to realise that, extraordinarily enough, it did not represent the way God loved. The pain, the suffering, the cruelty and poverty were not the point. They must be dealt with somehow, and they will be, given faith, quiet application and patience. But the love of God is outside and beyond any of this. It exists as much in a palace as in a hovel. It is of its nature open, uncritical, intemperate and that is what you must come to terms with. If you can. If you have the courage.

She came to love her neighbour, the human race, uncritically and intemperately herself, this earnest, not-very-bright, middleclass French girl. She wanted to give her life for it. 'This love of mine, how to show it?' she queries Marie, the old, early desperation resurfacing in the words. They didn't want her for a martyr, a missionary, an angel of mercy. 'Love needs to be proved by action.'

Indeed it does. But as you eventually came to understand, action proper to you, Thérèse of the Infant Jesus, a child forever, daughter of square old Louis the jeweller, confident little innocent, kicker of servants. Action such as only someone like you would dream of. *Allons, ma petite.* We are prepared. Give us the full bourgeois bit:

'Well, even a little child can scatter flowers, to scent the throne room with their fragrance: even a little child can sing, in its shrill treble, the great canticle of Love. That shall be my life, to scatter flowers – to miss no single opportunity of making some small sacrifice, here by a smiling look, there by a kindly word, always doing the tiniest things right, and doing it for love...

'I shall suffer all that I have to suffer – yes, and enjoy all my enjoyments too – in the spirit of love, so that I shall always be scattering flowers before God's throne: nothing that comes my way but shall yield up its petals. And as I scatter my flowers, I shall be singing: how could one be sad when occupied so pleasantly...?

'Jesus, I know that you will take pleasure in this fragrant shower of worthless petals, in these songs of love in which a worthless heart like mine sings itself out... And so the Church in heaven, ready to take part in the childish game I am playing, will begin scattering these flowers, now hallowed by your touch beyond all recognition: will scatter them on the souls in Purgatory... will scatter them on the Church Militant on earth...'

5.

Thérèse

and the

He and the She of it

Thérèse Martin came out of an all-female society, and progressed into an association of women that got along without men very successfully.

It was quite a skill, getting along without men at the end of the nineteenth century. Male power and authority was at its zenith. Women had no say in the governing of their nations, and their personal fortunes were often as not at the disposal of their husbands. The father of a family virtually ruled it. The Church for its part was a male institution, and in the case of the Catholic Church, a bachelor club. Severe and frequently grumpy humans who happened to be crested laid down the rules for others who had the effrontery to be cloven.

Women were not to be trusted, especially in matters pertaining to the intellect. Only men could be expected to think straight. When in 1898 Dom Madeleine, the first editor of *L'Histoire*, took the text to his bishop to recommend it for publication, he was initially warned off material proceeding from 'the imagination of women'. 27 years later, after the saint's canonisation, Pius XI signalled the gravity and unlikelihood of what he had just done by stating baldly 'St Thérèse of Lisieux is a great *man*, whose whole teaching is one of renunciation'.

Thérèse herself was lucky in the atmosphere within her family, because her father Louis was a teddy-bear. He was warm and affectionate, a good provider, a singer of songs and teller of tales, strict with his daughters but not domineering: just what a girl who thinks she knows where she's going needs. Her mother Zelie was sharper around the edges, a much stronger character – it was she who set the pattern of the girls' lives, sorted them out when they were difficult, saw to it they didn't go out dressed like that – but then she died early, which naturally enshrined her forever in a maternal forbearance which she did not quite possess. It is quite a good strategy to die young and serving your family devotedly if you wish your daughters to remember you as a mother as dedicated as any Sister of Charity.

Not that there was anything to say that Zelie was directly responsible for the rash of religious vocations that broke out in the Martin family. Yet she had wanted to take the veil herself as a young woman, and seems to have made no secret of the fact that marriage for her had been a second-best. Allegedly, she and Louis had initially entered into a 'chaste' marriage, after the manner of the fabled St Louis of France and his virgin bride. The practice was hardly widespread but not unknown in the Jansenist high noon: the notion was that you shared lives but not bedchambers. Zelie and Louis only weakened in their resolution after a (perhaps faintly envious) celibate priest irritably told them it was time they stopped playing pious games, and got on with it. Catholicism has arguably survived because of its hard core of unmarried clergy, seldom high-minded enough to see sexual abstinence as less than a deprivation.

Child-bearing was both the most rewarding and the most forbidding feature of nineteenth century marriage. A wife was expected to spend a long time having a lot of children, and the mortality rate for babies was heartbreakingly high (Zelie lost four of her nine children in infancy). The mortality rate for mothers themselves was hardly much better. The medical profession was getting round to making a separate discipline out of obstetrics, but for the time being there were only the village midwives and perhaps a rather dim GP in the background. As late as the 1860s at Guy's in London the therapy for women brought in with birth complications was to shave them bald-headed and pour foul-tasting purgatives down their throats. Things had not changed much since physicians cast devils out of women with labour problems in the Dark Ages.

The cloister went through its sociological permutations as an alternative female society. The fact that, down the centuries, orders of nuns were constantly having to be reformed probably indicates that women in different times and places simply made their own arrangements about 'the rule', and entered religious life to pursue a separate, more independent existence than they might have been offered outside the walls. (This does not mean they were then necessarily night-visited by grinning local yokels: Boccaccio-type scandals of course occurred, but for the majority of women who passed through the convent gates celibacy was an election and a relief.) The religious orders for their part seem to have understood well enough that wishing to be shot of men was a sufficient reason for a woman to enter the cloister.

When Thérèse and her sisters entered Carmel there was little need for reform, but there was certainly some for amelioration. It is impossible to say whether women make more eager penitents than men. Perhaps it is chauvinist to suggest that masochistic extremes seem historically to occur less frequently in male religious communities. Nineteenth century women in particular would have received from their mother's knee the notion that suffering in some form or other was their appointed lot, and when you have an enemy relentlessly bashing at the gates, you can either shrink away from him, or let him in and get it over with. In any event, Thérèse and her 'Little Way' did not hit the convents of

Christendom a moment too soon: it is possible to say her call to the religious life was precisely in order to knock a bit of sense into the heads of her sisters in Christ.

Convents of nuns always run their own temporal affairs, generally with minimal interference from Church authorities. This is not because the male brethren are less than interested where female religious are concerned, but because it is a brave bachelor who would willingly intervene in women's affairs. If some scatter-brained bursar reduces her institution to penury through carelessness and profligacy, that will be time enough for the luckless pooh-bah to step in and – ahem – remedy matters, but otherwise the exercise of a purely spiritual authority over female cloisters is as much as any wise cleric should covet.

Spiritual authority is a concealed weapon, however, it can in extreme cases be whipped out to terrorise a wayward community: in lesser situations used to regularise what may not truly be a fiercely irregular situation. It is a weapon invariably packed by men.

Men have (unfortunately, feminists will grate) always been necessary to female religious communities. Present-day Protestant churches are perhaps no longer constrained in the same way, but still under existing regulations in the Catholic Church it is impossible for the faithful to celebrate Mass or receive absolution in Penance (nowadays called the Sacrament of Reconciliation) without an ordained male to officiate. Yet the Mass, the Eucharist, is the very focus of a religious community's life, and Reconciliation the check or balance which, under God, empowers the pursuit of perfection. Nuns thus find themselves in the same position as Mrs Beeton and her jugged hare. They must first catch their priest.

Thérèse was acutely conscious of this problem in her own time. She was even more aware of it the wider her experience of religious life became. She saw that women had their own way of serving God, of loving God, but that their action was constantly being frustrated or modified by male insight. New congregations of nuns could not even decide about the rule of life they would follow: the patriarchal Holy Office would have the last word on that. (It is interesting that the old code of canon law had only five or six pages of legislation relating to religious orders of men, but 20 to 30 concerning religious orders of women. Never the twain shall meet, between us and them there is fixed, etc.)

Like Goggins in *Handy Andy* the nineteenth century Church found women 'troublesome cattle to deal with', and responded by fencing them in, ordering their byres, and training monsignori to yap at their heels when they wouldn't get into the pasture as they were supposed to. Having run across yet another notice forbidding women entry, or requiring specific dress of them, during her grand tour of Christian Europe, Thérèse finally got entirely fed up with the attitude:

'... I still can't understand why it's so easy for a woman to get excommunicated in Italy! All the time, people seemed to be saying: "No, you mustn't go here, you mustn't go there, you'll be excommunicated". There's no respect for us poor wretched women anywhere. And yet you'll find the love of God much commoner among women than among men, and the women at the Crucifixion showed much more courage than the Apostles, exposing themselves to insult, wiping our Lord's face. I suppose he lets us share the neglect he himself chose for his lot on this earth: in heaven, where the last shall be first, we shall know more about what God thinks...'

Thérèse thought she knew about what God thought. Or she hoped she did. After all, the greatest frustration of her life was that, being female, she could not be a priest. And that was what she felt herself most powerfully called to be.

It was a certain vocation as far as she was concerned. She believed herself so surely chosen to bring Jesus to others in the form of the sacraments that for a while she went through a period of bitter resentment for not having been born a boy. Yet even when she got over that (and sulks never lasted long with her), she could still become a little unbalanced about the fact that conventual life was all that appeared to be open to a mere female. Why?

'... I feel as if I'd got the courage to be a Crusader, a Pontifical Zouave, dying on the battlefield in defence of the Church! And at the same time I want to be a priest: how lovingly I'd carry you (she is engaged in an apostrophe) in my hands when you came down from heaven at my call, how lovingly I'd bestow you upon men's souls. And yet with all this desire to be a priest, I've nothing but admiration and envy for the humility of St Francis: I'd willingly imitate him in refusing the honour of the priesthood...'

The saint of Assisi had been ordained a deacon, but then 'out of respect' had declined to take priestly orders. Thérèse understood that. For her, as for all of her time and persuasion, the office she craved seemed a superlative dignity. Catholics to the present day think of priesthood as something a bit more than mere ministry. Ordination, in catechism-speak, imposes a 'character' on the soul. Doubtless the holy awe has been laid on too thick down the years, and in certain regions in the past has combined with social factors to produce distinctly unfortunate results. But for all that, the priest is dubbed 'another Christ' when the Bishop lays hands on him, and a woman like Thérèse would devoutly have accepted that to be stunningly true.

Thus she too aspired to be another Christ. In her own case she was not constrained by the (faintly spurious, when you come to think of it) humility of St Francis. It could even be that the priesthood had need of the likes of her:

'Another discovery I made: about priests. I'd never been in close touch with them, and I'd been puzzled by that phrase in the Rule about the chief object for which the Reformed Carmelites exist. Pray for sinners by all means, but why priests? Surely their souls were like flawless crystal already: it bothered me...

'Well, that journey to Italy justified itself, if only by throwing a sidelight on my vocation. (The tour with Louis and Céline.) I mean, I lived for a month among a lot of good and holy priests, and came to realise that although their high office makes them rank above the angels, they have their frailties and their weaknesses like other men. And these were good and holy priests, "the salt of the earth": if such people need our prayers, and need them badly, what about the priests who have gone slack...?'

What, indeed. A question was beginning to form in her mind which, as a pious daughter of her time, she hardly dared ask. Might not devout women themselves fulfil the office of presbyter, rather than simply wearing out hassocks on behalf of their often flawed brothers? Might not a woman be 'priested', at the very least to bring the sacred mysteries to her sisters within the female enclosure? Why should there be the constant dependence upon a seconded male, basically unfamiliar with, perhaps even alien to, the emotional and spiritual problems of a cloistered sisterhood?

There was only one priest that Thérèse ever truly got on with in her years in Carmel. His name was Père Pichon, and he was a Jesuit who eventually went off to be a missionary in Canada. But he seems to have had an immediate insight into Thérèse's soul. She was somewhat taken aback by this, but none the less loud in her grateful acknowledgement:

'... he told me that he was astonished at God's dealings with my soul: he'd been looking at me the evening before when I was praying in choir, and got the impression that my fervour was still the fervour of childhood, and the way by which I was being led was one of unruffled calm. Then he added: "You must thank God for the mercy he's shown you: if he left you to yourself, you wouldn't be a little angel any longer, you'd be a little demon."...'

One can see her blanching at that, gulping to think that he had penetrated to the naughty kiddibunk within. So to say, he was challenging her to live down to her own lack of pretension. In the event she responded just like a good girl should: 'I'd no difficulty believing that: I knew how weak and imperfect I was... Some other words of his remain deeply imprinted on my heart too: "My child, there's one Superior, one Novice master you must always obey – Jesus Christ"...'

Now this was the wink as good as a nod for

gamine Thérèse. It can be seen with hindsight as probably the most valuable piece of advice anybody ever gave her. For some time she had been thinking that 'spiritual direction' was a great waste of time. For some reason or other she found it difficult to 'open out' to others – even to Pichon – and whenever she managed partially to do so (generally with her Mother Superior or a senior nun), she found what she gained in return was not worth the effort. The females tended only to echo the males who had shaped them. And as for them, harrumphing away behind their confessional grilles: heavens to Hildegarde of Tubingen, weren't they all so lost in their masculine conceits that they simply couldn't get hold of the notion of Jesus' little playmate playing prayer games in the nursery?

She developed her notion of being a toy that the baby Jesus sometimes amused himself with, sometimes cast aside into a corner. It is still for many her juvenilia at its most shudderingly ingenuous. Yet it was her way of saying that she was browned off with what passed for spiritual guidance in her life, and was looking to another source. 'I turned to him who is the Director of all those entrusted with the direction of souls,' she writes with a touch of triumphalism, 'and learned from him that secret which he hides from the wise and prudent, and reveals only to little children...'

So there, again. And that, extraordinarily, was the way it was from then on for this most notable Catholic saint of modern times. She couldn't be a priest herself, but she could do without the old drears who were busy making a male province of the job. She thus afterwards conformed externally to the rules and practices of her Catholic life, but kept an ear out for Jesus himself rather than his representatives. The Protestants would have hailed her as recruited to their cause. The Catholics would have fled from her as a self-willed deviant. In a sense she was both, and neither.

Her spiritual life found its own, or rather God's, level. She automatically looked to female models rather than male among the saints, choosing St Cecilia and St Joan of Arc as special patronesses. They may appear faintly eccentric models, but in fact each of them shows forth an important aspect of Thérèse the child-woman.

To take Cecilia first, not much is known about her except that she was a martyr who died because she would not consummate her forced marriage to a pagan, and is the patron saint of music because as the organ wheezed out *O Promise Me* or its ancient Roman equivalent at her unconsenting nuptials, she 'sang in her heart to the Lord'. Thérèse and Céline went to visit her supposed tomb in the Catacombs when they were in Rome. Thérèse claimed 'a real bond of friendship' with Cecilia...

'She became a favourite, a confidante, to whom I entrusted my secrets. Everything about her attracted me, but above all the way she gave herself up into God's hands, the boundless confidence which enabled her to inspire souls hitherto so fond of worldly enjoyments with her own ideal of virginity. St Cecilia reminds me of the bride in the Canticles: "a song in an armed camp" is a good description of her. Her whole life was a melodious song that rose above all the trials she endured: and no wonder, because she "carried the holy gospel printed on her heart" – her heart, in which the divine Lover had found a resting place...'

She is here writing more hagiography than she ever read. Cecilia seems essentially to represent for Thérèse the virginity which was so much a part of her character, the hallmark of her specific femininity. Thérèse valued physical integrity because it was for her the earnest of enduring innocence. Little children are aware of their sexuality principally as something that individualises them. One is a 'girl' or a 'boy' just as one is English or French. Thus for Thérèse, Cecilia is the symbol of the pure little girl. It is that pristine freshness, rather than virginity in the sense of the sacrifice of sexual activity, that she wishes to offer to her divine Lover. And of course Cecilia is also the 'song in an armed camp': which brings us neatly to Joan of Arc.

Joan was a French heroine, who took her cue from her voices in prayer, and ventured forth with fire and sword to defend her country against its oppressors. She represents a Thérèse who would have liked to exist, but couldn't quite: a Thérèse who by some unlikely genetic fluke might have emerged as a martyr or a missionary. (Or a Salvation Army captain: in her military/soul-saving mood she can remind one powerfully of Catherine Booth.)

Her father Louis was *un bon Français*, and Thérèse was certainly nothing if not French. But in fact patriotism, however sincerely felt, was in the context just grist to her mill. What she writes about Joan is more complex than anything to do with national pride or love of country:

'... the only true glory, I soon learned to realise, is the glory that lasts forever: and to win that, you don't need to perform any dazzling exploits – you want to live a hidden life, doing good in such an unobtrusive way that you don't even let your left hand know what your right hand is doing. That happened, for example, when I read stories about heroic French women like the Venerable Joan of Arc (Joan was not at this point canonised, but her 'cause had been introduced': thus Thérèse gives her her precise title, however on the retired list it makes her sound), who loved their country so well. How I longed to imitate them: how strong it seemed to beat in me, this heroic ardour of theirs, the sense of divine inspiration!

'And it was in this connection that a great grace came to me: the greatest, I always think, I have ever received in my life – because in those days I seldom had those lights in prayer which latterly have been so showered on me. I felt that I was born for greatness: but when I asked myself how I was to achieve it, God put into my mind that ideal which I've just mentioned...'

We have been here before. Thérèse came to know quite clearly that she would be a saint. It is a trick that only the truly holy can pull off. (Humility is truth.) But here Joan of Arc gets the credit (or blame) for revealing Thérèse's destiny to her, and also for showing her that the means of her sanctification is to be the 'Little Way'. It is the lion lying down with the lamb.

One may validly ask just how such an essentially gentle, non-violent person as Thérèse came to be so attracted to Joan of Arc. The brutality and swagger of war, with which Joan lived – and with which in some sense she must have empathised – was a long day's march from anything to do with Thérèse. Yet it has already been noted that her devotion to our Lady centred on *Notre Dame des Victoires*, which is really just the Mother of God in French battledress. One allows of course that Thérèse was a bland innocent in the area. Prussians had stalked through Alencon in 1871, looting and terrorising the inhabitants, imperilling Louis and Zelie and their young family, but that had conveniently been before Thérèse's birth. There do not seem to have been any military men nor tradition of service in her family. She did not of course like playing with dolls in the nursery. It may be as simple as that at some point she fixated on tin soldiers.

It is a question for many today of whether Thérèse, had she lived in our time, would have taken up arms in the battle for women priests.

It is important, because many Catholic women's groups, dismayed that there are now women priests and ministers in other Christian churches but as yet none in their own, have begun to adopt Thérèse as their patroness. Some publicly hail her as the 'Inspirer and Forerunner of the Ministry of Women'. It seems true to say Thérèse would have relished buckling on the armour in this cause. But then after a little while she might have puckered her brow and wondered what the row was all about.

She was no good in a gang. She disliked 'joining', and the abstracts of justice and equality that lead so many people to band together and storm the barricades would probably have baffled her. She had simply seen no reason in her lifetime why she should not have been a priest. She once came across a pious legend to the effect that Stanislaus Koztka, the sainted Jesuit novice, had when he was very ill been brought the Eucharist by St Barbara. 'Why not an angel,' Thérèse demands in a letter, miffed and personally piqued, 'or a priest – but a simple maiden? I imagine that those who have desired it on earth shall in heaven enjoy the privileges of the priesthood...'

And when she was on her deathbed, she managed to breathe that she was glad to be dying at the age of 24 (the canonical age for ordination), because it meant 'the good God spares me the sorrow of living without ever being a priest...'

Granted somebody else played Joan of Arc, Thérèse would probably not have been averse to a series of planned attacks on the chancelleries and bishops' palaces of Christendom. She had once after all patted her horse's neck and charged the papal throne itself. This was when she was in Rome, desperate to enter Carmel at the early age of 15, and had confronted the gaunt and severe Leo XIII in the *Sala dei Palafrenieri*.

The occasion had been Leo's Jubilee, and part of the reason for the pilgrimage to Rome was so that the devout citizens of the diocese of Bayeux might present the Pope with the gift of a lace rochet in Louis XIV style, embroidered with the papal arms as well as those of various Norman cities. This was to happen after a Mass which Leo would celebrate for them in the Consistorial Hall. Devotions safely under their belt, the pilgrims were introduced to the Pope, filing past him in his white cassock and zucchetta, seated in his big armchair.

'... I got a general impression of cardinals and archbishops and bishops standing round him,' writes Thérèse, dry-mouthed, 'but I didn't try to distinguish them because I had eyes for nothing but the Holy Father himself. We passed before him one by one, each pilgrim kneeling, kissing first his foot and then his hand, and receiving his benediction: then two members of the noble guard touched him lightly on the shoulder as a warning to get up – touched the pilgrim, I mean, not the Pope: how badly I tell me story...'

She was rattled again. Playing grown-up games always bothered her. The pilgrims had been left in no doubt that it was utterly forbidden to speak to the Pope. Before his Holiness appeared in the *Sala*, the Vicar General of Bayeux, instructed by his bishop, had told them in loud French (so there could be no possible misunderstanding) that they were simply meant to get in there, make their quick salaam, and get out. That was to be the complete scene. There would be no holding up the queue, no messing. Thérèse swallowed heavily, her heart beating faster than it had done in the Colosseum.

'Before I went in, I had fully resolved to speak out: but my courage began to desert me when I found M. Reverony, of all people (the Vicar General himself), standing close to his right hand... I turned round to consult dear Céline, and she said "Speak out". A moment later, there I was at the Holy Father's feet, kissing his shoe: but when he held out his hand, I clasped mine together and looked up at him with tears starting to my eyes: "Most Holy Father," I said, "I've a great favour to ask of you." He bent towards me till his head was nearly touching my face, and his dark, deep-set eyes seemed to look right down into the depths of my soul. "Most Holy Father," I said, "in honour of your jubilee, I want you to let me enter the Carmelite order at fifteen"...

There was doubtless the hiss of escaping breath stage right, but the Pope seemed a little confused.

120

It was not that he had not heard Thérèse's husky request, but the demand was so curious as to appear unlikely. He looked to M. Reverony. 'I can't quite understand,' he murmured. Reverony in his turn swallowed hard, and summoned up all his gravitas. 'This child here,' he pronounced, and one can hear the emphasis on child, 'is anxious to enter Carmel at 15, and her superiors are looking into the matter at the moment...'

It was the right answer, because the Church, like the government, depends on a stout bureaucracy to keep its wheels oiled. Given that the right committee has been set up, there is no need for any action whatever to be taken. 'Very well, my child,' assented the Pope, relaxed again, looking back to Thérèse, 'do what your superiors tell you.' But Thérèse wasn't having that one. She had not been a Catholic for years without having twigged that if you just smile and get in line, you find yourself shoved away in a sacristy cupboard and locked in. 'Yes, but if you would just say the word, Most Holy Father,' she protested in a louder tone, grasping his knees, 'everybody would agree.'

M. Reverony was now wriggling to get his hands on this uppity female. Though of tender years, she was a woman, and had touched the person of the Pontiff. Surely that merited another of those excommunications reserved to her sex. If not, a committee would have to be set up to look into the matter. But the Pope decided to live with it. 'All's well, all's well,' he consoled the now volubly weeping girl, 'if God wants you to enter, you will.'

She had got through to the source of power, but she was apparently not going to finish up with half of anybody's kingdom, let alone the head of John the Baptist. '...his kindness gave me courage,' she sobs out, 'and I wanted to go on: but two members of the noble guard, finding that I paid no attention to their ceremonial touch, took me by the arms, and M. Reverony helped them to lift me up (sic, a thousand times sic): I kept my arms on the Pope's knees, and they had to carry me away by main force. As they did so, His Holiness put his hand to my lips, and then raised it in blessing: he followed me with his eyes for a long time...'

Her tears did not cease as she was dragged out, nor for some little time after. Even Leo XIII probably had to think that she was a bit over the top for the usual young hysteric confronted by the Pope. Yet there is no evidence that he ever mentioned the matter to anyone subsequently, nor gave it serious thought. But the fact is that Thérèse did enter Carmel when she was just 15 and 3 months, on April 18, 1888, so the attack on the male ecclesiastical establishment in Rome must be judged as successful as Joan's capture of Orleans.

The only difference was scale. But doing things in a small way was Thérèse's stock-in-trade. She did not think any action contemptible because it was hardly worth doing. It took quite as much resolution to be nice to an old bat who flung soapy water in your face as to march into a city and kick the invaders out. Anyway, what more was a little girl capable of? And a little girl she was. And meant to remain.

The fact that she was a girl was arguably more important than that she was little. There is a sense in which the 'Little Way' is a spirituality designed for women, and has its drawbacks where men are concerned. It needs to be put in other terms to succeed. This was independently achieved, oddly enough, by a Frenchman who preceded Thérèse by a few years, Jean Claude Colin, the founder of the Society of Mary, or Marist Fathers. Colin would in the typical masculine way no doubt have thrown up at the notion of the toy the baby Jesus shoves to one side, but he set as the ideal for his followers that they should be *ignotus et quasi occultus* (unknown and as it were hidden). This was the 'Little Way' writ macho.

Thérèse was so much the little girl that when she entered Carmel, she did not want to lose her childish name. Nuns of all orders in those days took another appellation to signify that they had left their 'old life' behind, and thus could easily finish up Sr Philibert of the Sacred Passion or Sr Radegund of the Seven Sorrows. Thérèse had thought about it a lot while she was still at home, aware that it could turn into a serious problem:

'... Carmel had its Teresa of Jesus already, and yet it wouldn't do to give up the name of Thérèse, such a lovely name. And all at once I remembered my devotion to the Sacred Infancy, and thought how wonderful it would be to be called Thérèse of the Child Jesus. I didn't say anything about this daydream of mine: but sure enough, when dear Mother Marie Gonzague asked the sisters what I was to be called, this dream-name of mine was the one they thought of. How pleased I was! It looked like a special favour from the Child Jesus, this happy piece of thought transference...'

Well, it was a funny coincidence. Her sister nuns appear to have seen at once that a little girl was coming into their midst, and had decided to signalise the fact. She was to be a child forever among them. Her content knew no bounds at the time: but it is interesting to speculate on how long it might have lasted, and how an inevitable maturing might have altered her understanding the world and of the 'he and the she of it'. A woman would find it hard to go on being a little flower waiting for Jesus to pick her once she is 40, and the lines of the face have deepened.

Had she lived, Thérèse as an adult would arguably have been ahead of her time on many of the issues affecting women. She would almost certainly have seen the point of married women pursuing a career, for example. Her own mother had done as much, and young and 'clumsy' Thérèse must have envied her skill at *Point d'Alencon*. Examples of Zelie's work adorned the Martin house for long after her death, reminding her girls that if they had a gift, it was not to be neglected.

Thérèse saw her ability to pray as a gift: even had she married rather than entered Carmel, that would not have gone to waste. She wondered too if her writing was not a gift, and did as much as she could to develop it. On balance her style remains only adequate, but that is not the point. There are many who do not admire Enid Blyton or Barbara Cartland, but who still acknowledge them as formidable achievers.

Thérèse as an enclosed nun would also surely have applauded the suffragettes. She would have been highly discreet and private about it, however, because the last thing a Reformed Carmelite was supposed to do was speak out on a public issue. But she had seen enough of the Church to know that women in any condition were in need of a voice and representation. Ironically, representation was an advantage she enjoyed as an enclosed nun. Within Carmel, Superiors were elected by the professed members for a fixed number of years. Any Messalina who clawed her way to the top could securely be got rid of at the next general chapter. David Copperfield's mother and many a Victorian wife, in thrall their Mr Murdstone, might have wondered who precisely was making the noble sacrifice.

Asked to express a view, Thérèse would obviously have supported 'equality in the workplace'. She had ground too many teeth to the gums putting up with unsuitable/untalented males in cassocks to have any patience with notions of male supremacy. The person best equipped to do the job, whatever his/her sex or race, would have struck her as an excellent *tendance*. While she might well have gone along with the ontological understanding of her time – the man the 'head' of the woman – she would still have required this to be understood in charity. In other words, if a man found a woman more capable than himself, then it was his business to step down and make way for her. God has the disposition of gifts, and we are not to tell God his business.

A non-proscriptive attitude was the hallmark of her spirituality in every department. Thus there was no sense in which she would ever have hated or despised men, even when it appeared to her that men did little but stand in her light. She was never a feminist in the sense of one who went out collecting society's dirty washing, humping it back to the tubs, rolling up her sleeves, and getting on with the scrubbing.

You got splashed doing that. And look what that did to your solidarity with your sisters.

6.

Thérèse
and Authority

Thérèse of Lisieux is generally put forward as a model of docility and obedience. Bishops, priests, abbots, mothers superior, and just plain mothers fed up with their rebellious broods, laud her as precisely the sort of pliable subject they were thinking of when they took on their arduous responsibilities in the first place. (Nobody in religious life seeks or welcomes power over others, it is to be understood: it is a heavy cross, taken up solely for the sake of the brethren.)

Thérèse not only obeyed the rule scrupulously, but she actually enjoyed being corrected for minor breaches. She so often kissed the floor in token of submission to her superiors, some of her sisters must have thought she suffered from curvature of the spine. She was so far from resentment at being told what to do that she would interpret even a patently stupid order as regrettably too sensible for a thicko like her to understand.

Heavens to Teresa of Avila and all saintly patrons of the religious life.

There has, as I indicate, been a campaign to promote Thérèse as superhumanly submissive. A male celibate clergy has a particular dread of stroppy nuns. So the fact that Thérèse was remarkably precise in her observance of the Carmelite rule has, in a sense, been used against her. She has been turned into an icon of the uncomplaining votary. Yet the reason why she conformed so faithfully to even finicky custom and practice within Carmel (how to fold your habit at night, how to place your cutlery when you finished eating, etc.) is not properly appreciated.

She seriously thought herself dangerously self-willed and too fond of her own way, and as a consequence believed she stood in compelling need of a tight rein.

The odd thing is that she was in her way half right about this. It was seldom observable, but there was a festering individualism deep down in Thérèse. Zelie observed a greater stubbornness and resolution in her youngest daughter than in any of the others, and worried about it. 'Baby,' she writes in an early letter to her sister, 'when things aren't going well for her, gets pitiably worked up, so that I have to talk her round: she seems to think that all is lost, and sometimes the feeling is too much for her, and she chokes with indignation...' Thérèse puts it rather more ominously: 'With a nature like mine, I might have turned out thoroughly wicked, and perhaps lost my soul...'

To lose one's soul was the enduring dread of Christians a century ago. Perdition loomed. You could slip unsuspecting into mortal sin. A belief in predestination may have been forbidden to Catholics, but pervasive Jansensim saw to it that everybody remembered that the gate was strait and the way narrow. Thérèse in best childish form once thought of freely offering herself for Hell, the abode of the lost, so that there would be at least one creature in that *ultima thule* who loved her Maker. But that was perhaps because she thought she could be headed that way anyhow in spite of herself. It was a curious and inconsistent appreciation of the Divine Justice. She understood that her upbringing had been both very strict and distressingly pampered.

The pampering came from Louis. Had Zelie lived, Thérèse might have been subjected to a rather more rigid rule of life. Louis was a precise and observant man, who would never for a moment have countenanced laxity in Thérèse (and whom Thérèse for her part would never have dreamed of wounding), but for all that her lightest wish was his command. He was besotted with his little girl. Father and daughter had a little fantasy, that he should be King of France and Navarre. and she should be his Queen.

This meant in practice that the King did whatever the Queen wanted. There was seldom any argument. The whole thing might well have been a shrewd ploy worked out by a manipulative child.

There is indeed no saying how deliberate was Thérèse's management of her father. It is clear enough that had she been subject to other, more malign influences, the whole thing might have had the most unfortunate consequences. She had an ornery streak beneath the sugar and spice, and authority may well have appealed to her in the first place as something to be controlled, rather than respected and obeyed.

She learned early how to handle men. It was men after all who weilded the power in her world. Yet if only you pricked them in the right spot their natural pomposity leaked away. Tears were a girl's best friend. (By an unintended irony, she refers to them throughout the autobiography as her 'diamonds'.) Louis succumbed immediately to the bright glitter in her eye, and his daughter had found that priests and even bishops – and no doubt politicians, heads of state, if ever it should come to it – were equally susceptible.

When she was 14 and agitating to enter Carmel, Thérèse went with Louis to Bayeux to see M. Reverony, the Vicar General of the diocese, whom she was later to cross over speaking to the Pope in Rome. Reverony knew already of Thérèse's ambition to be a nun, but at this point had had a fairly low opinion of her. He was consequently short with the young petitioner and her father, merely saying he would take them to see the Bishop, to whom Thérèse should make out whatever case she thought she could present. Thérèse allowed her 'diamonds' to show at this, but Reverony had somewhere learned a thing or two about young females: stop that, was his sharp command, his Lordship wouldn't like to see that.

So Thérèse saved it up. No sense casting your diamonds before the assistant pawnbroker. The Bishop was discovered in a long gallery several 'enormous' rooms away. Thérèse describes herself as feeling no bigger than an ant *chez eveque*, and was installed in a chair 'big enough for four people of my size'. (It is extraordinary, looking back on it, in what style even comparitively humble church dignitaries once contrived to live.) Thérèse had put her hair up to try and look older than she was, so she was quickly intimidated when the Bishop suggested that really, oughtn't she as a young girl to be thinking of her widowed father rather than romanticizing in this silly fashion about religious life? There was, he said, in fact not a lot he could do about her odd desire to be a Carmelite before he had had a conference with the Cure of St Jacques (the 'ecclesiastical superior' of the Lisieux convent). Thérèse bit her lip interiorly at this:

'... this was the worst news I could have had: I was up against a brick wall there. Regardless of what M. Reverony had said, I not only let his Lordship see the diamonds in my eyes, I treated him to a shower of them. He was touched, I could see that: he put his arm round my neck and let my head rest upon his shoulders, petting me with a fondness he's never shown, I was told, for anyone else...'

That was more like it. The Bishop was behaving as a normal male should. That M. Reverony was simply cold and hard-hearted. And the ploy worked, though it took its time: it was this same Bishop of Bayeux who a year later issued the dispensation that enabled Thérèse to enter Carmel at 15, just as she had desired. There had had to be the petting, of course. *Mais alors*, this was business. Interestingly, the Bishop claimed his little *quid pro quo* for some time after. Thérèse drops gently into the narrative, writing of the day on which she was clothed a Carmelite:

'... after the ceremony, the Bishop came in, and showed me all the kindness of a father: he was really proud, I think, of my perseverance, and described me everywhere as his little daughter. It was always like that when he came to visit the convent: I remember especially the day he came to us for the centenary of St John of the Cross. He took my head between his hands and petted me in all sorts of ways: I had never felt so honoured...'

'Honoured' shows that Thérèse, like all those with the ornery streak deep down, could 'creep' when she felt she had to. She was an innocent, but hardly a fool. She must have known the Bishop was simply up to the old male celibate trick of flirting with juveniles because you could hardly try it on with mature women. The guileless Little Flower had a canny attitude towards superiors which we shall have to come back to. It is hard not to judge that she was less than straightforward in many of her dealings with the religious executive.

Strictly spiritual authority was of course something else again. Thérèse never tried to twist her directors and guides around her little finger. In fact they were no more worth the manipulation than they were the soul-baring. 'God meant to deal with me personally, without making use of any intermediary,' she observes a touch winsomely more than once.

The Church itself she saw as a sort of magic mountain of authority. There was a mystic quality in the way it dispensed teaching and practice. It was Holy Mother Church, which made its blind spot about women a bit peculiar, but there were consolations. The Church ratified and authenticated the Holy Relics, for instance, making it possible for the humble faithful to honour the dear saints as they wished to. Thérèse was very keen on honouring Holy Relics. But she appreciated that such devotion could easily decline into superstition, and thus sought official sanction for whatever veneration she singled out.

The cult of relics is one of the more dubious by-ways of Catholicism. Most people can accept that you may wish to keep a souvenir of those who have gone before you on the mantel shelf, but hardly their detached fingers or toes. (Or head, in the case of John the Baptist: has anyone ever looked inside that reliquary in the English church in Rome?) In Thérèse's time the cult of relics was at an emotional peak. The mortal remains of the saints were thought to testify to the resurrection, and so it was worth going a long way and undergoing immense discomfort to whisper into the embalmed ear of St Alphonsus (a renowned confessor) or hear inner promptings from the mummified tongue of St Antony (a popular preacher).

Thérèse herself can only be described as punting happily along with the stream. She liked to bring back a personal memento from every holy place she visited – a scoop of dust from the Catacombs, a chip of stone from the church of St Agnes in Rome. Eventually her bedroom at Les Buissonnets became cluttered with pious detritus which she alone could identify.

Over the Holy House of Loreto (transported from Nazareth by angels, set down in northern Italy just where you could build a cathedral over it), she went spare. 'How deeply I was moved,' she writes fervently, 'to share the same roof, as it were, with the Holy Family... To have seen the little room in which the angel greeted her (Mary), to have put down my rosary beads for a moment in the bowl from which the Child Jesus had eaten – those are things you can't remember without a thrill...'

Just as the Bishop went hook, line and sinker for Thérèse, so Thérèse fell Miraculous Medal and all for devotional *ackamaracka*. She had no difficulty in accepting objects as authentic if the Church said they were. (Actually, as the boring old monsignori were constantly pointing out, the Church never said they were: it just declined to say they necessarily weren't.) She liked to touch 'holy things', as though contact brought her closer to their originators. It was at this juncture incidentally that she turned bolshie about the unbiquitous notices threatening censure for any such temerity. At Holy Cross in Rome:

> '... we venerated several relics of the true Cross, as well as two of the Thorns and the Nails, all enclosed in a magnificent gold reliquary with no glass in it. So when my turn came I managed to put my finger through one of the holes, and actually touched one of the Nails which had been bathed in the Precious Blood. Was it presumptuous of me? Well, God sees into the depths of our hearts, and he knew that my intentions were good, that I'd have done anything rather than offend him. I claimed the privileges of a child, that doesn't bother about asking leave, but treats all its Father's treasures as if they were its own...'

It is the attitude of a little Queen confident that her King will always understand and co-operate. Thérèse of course did not live long enough to encounter the researches of an aged Jesuit in Paris, who in the 1920s added together all the authenticated pieces of the True Cross in the world, and came up with a structure about the size of the Arc de Triomphe. Whether he also worked out how many Nails and Thorns bathed in the Precious Blood there were in circulation is not recorded, but the so-called Mafiosi Monks of Mazzarino were at one stage selling off job lots of each commodity, so a warehouseful would not seem an excessive estimate.

Thérèse needed to believe in relics, because they brought the realities of her faith closer to her: something of which she stood in constant need. She was not 'weak in faith', and suffered comparitively few doubts in the real sense of the word (save at the very end of her life, when her gross sufferings caused her to fear that God had abandonned her), but as a mere juvenile in a disastrously grown-up world, she needed constant reassurance. The kiss of the Child Jesus imprinted on the incorrupt body of St Catherine of Sienna (which Thérèse venerated in Bologna, the cheeky student successfully banished from her thoughts) gave you precisely that. It made you think that poverty, chastity and obedience were worthwhile crosses to bear: especially the heaviest of them all, obedience.

Though she never articulated them or allowed them to challenge her dedication, Thérèse had problems with obedience. She valued her liberty dearly, as her young wilfulness and organizing behaviour with Louis had shown, but in Carmel she appeared to have given it away through what might in the long run prove to have been a parlous fear. 'Hadn't I begged him (Jesus) to take my liberty away,' she writes reflectively, 'because I was afraid of the use I might make of it: hadn't I longed, weak and helpless as I was, to be united once for all with that divine Strength...?'

It was protesting too much. Why should she be afraid of the use she might make of her liberty when as a happy-go-lucky child she could only esteem it as God's most precious gift to her? She had a natural attraction to chastity, and poverty was no problem to her: she had always been content with whatever was put on the table, and she had never had any true desire for possessions, at home or in Carmel. But obedience did cramp one's style. She was not used to being constrained at every turn. A child likes working out her own games and playing them without hindrance.

Religious obedience is meant to curb self-will and free from the tyranny of desire. It is disliked by those who do not share its ideals for two reasons. It concentrates too much power in what may well be incompetent hands (the superiors), and it removes responsibility for their actions from those who recklessly hand over their freedom to the putative chumps who arbitrarily outrank them.

It does seem odd, in a world whose history has been very largely an ongoing battle for basic human liberties, that people should ever have seen it as virtuous to subject their wills to another fallible mortal. There would not seem to be any special merit in doing what somebody else tells you, just because it is an order in a religious context, and just because the superior is alleged to 'stand in the place of God' while issuing it. Even soldiers are supposed to think before they obey a command from a lawful superior. Indeed in one of the broadcasts which led to his murder in El Salvador, Oscar Romero defined it as the duty of the military man to weigh his actions before embarking on them. Religious obedience may thus be seen as a simple cop-out.

Thérèse perhaps in fact did see it as someting of a cop-out, but suppressed the knowledge. She could not face up to mistakes of this nature: it was too disillusioning. Yet her expressed fear of her own liberty is arguably just a way of her saying that, boil it down, she is better off not making decisions herself. As with friendship at school, the whole thing looks damn tricky, and she is better shot of it.

It is important to impress again that there was no alternative for an independent-minded Catholic young woman of Thérèse's day to either marriage or the convent. The Brontes may have managed to sit tight in their father's rectory and write their books, but then they were talented persons (as Thérèse never thought she was for a moment), and the kind who would probably have done what they had to do anyway. Thérèse knew herself to be just a dim little soul. Yet it was not in her nature to do anything by halves. So it was better, she imagined, that her personal liberty should be completely taken away from her. Better the Rule and Reverend Mother should say when she should stand, sit, pray, sleep, write poetry. You never knew, it might work. In religious life there were Prioresses who increased the life of grace within you as well as old bats who made you wonder was it going on at all.

Mother Marie de Gonzague (three times Thérèse's Prioress) has already been described as an old bat, and that is precisely what she was. In the world she had been the well-born Marie Adele Rosalie Davy de Vircille, and in religion never quite forgot it. She and her kind had been born to lead. The bourgeoisie were the salt of the earth, of course, but their blood was something else. You never knew where it had been.

It would be absurd to suggest that the conflict between Thérèse and Mother Marie de Gonzague came down to class war. But conflict between the two women there certainly was, and it cannot have helped that they came from opposite sides of the tracks. Thérèse's ideas about religious life were less than traditional. Marie de Gonzague for her part was a confirmed roller in nettles. She thus quickly began to see herself as the keeper of the flame *vis-a-vis* Thérèse. A regimen of unyeilding strictness would have to be imposed on this unformed and possibly dangerous young entrant into Carmel.

It soon became a species of persecution for Thérèse. Marie de Gonzague was determined and insensitive as only those burdened with coronets can be. Thérèse reacted as she had done with the bishop of Bayeux: by crawling. It is a nasty word, and perhaps in the end represents a harsh judgement. She was so young for the intensity of Carmel, and anyway so childish in intent, that it could simply have been that she was cowed in spite of herself. But for all that, her writing reveals an innate servility, and it leaves a bad taste in the mouth:

'... I know she (the Prioress) was very fond of me, and said the nicest things about me: but God saw to it that she should treat me very severely without meaning to. I hardly ever met her without having to kiss the ground in penance for something I'd done wrong...

'This was a grace beyond all price: quite unmistakably, God was acting like this through his earthly representative. I don't know what would have become of me if I'd been treated as the pet of the community... Instead of learning to see my superiors as the expression of our Lord's will, I might have become interested in them as persons, and so my heart, which had always been fancy-free when I was in the world, might have been entangled by human attachments in the cloister...'

It is hard to divorce oneself from the fact that the author of these words knew a woman who had made life a trial for her was one day probably going to read them, and needed to be buttered up in case she was still in office. Hidden in the passage is also the suggestion that if there had been any justice in the world, Thérèse should have been the pet of the community. She would certainly have known where she was in that case.

Being the 'pet' was a situation she was used to,

and it would have enabled her to deal with the intransigents of Carmel (there were others as well as Marie de Gonzague) much as she had dealt with Louis. She also seems curiously to claim that she had been without ties of affection in the world, but lay 'in danger' of them in Carmel. What she surely means here is that in her family her affections had been clear and reciprocated, whereas in the convent she found herself a poor lost lamb, unsure even that she was truly welcome in the fold. If she was not to be the adored baby to her sisters, what was she to be?

Her natural sisters were in Carmel of course, and that helped. A new day began to dawn on the enclosure for Thérèse when Pauline was elected Prioress. This was in 1893, when the youngest Martin had been in Carmel for four years. She had not expected Pauline's advancement, and was over the moon. Adressing her sister (Mother Agnes of Jesus) in the first part of *L'Histoire*, she sings:

> '... God is more tender to us than any mother could be, and you, Mother, are always ready to forgive those little indiscretions of which I am guilty without meaning to be. Again and again I have found that a single caress from you has had more effect on me than any reprimand you could have uttered...
>
> 'This feeling that love was winging my feet has been with me specially since that golden day when you were elected Prioress – that Pauline should stand in my life for our Lord's representative! Not

that I hadn't realized, for a long time, what wonderful things our Lord was doing through your influence...'

The whole passage is shouting sucks to the old bat. A new Prioress was elected for three years, which provided plenty of time to hang new wallpaper and get the toy box reorganized. Yet Pauline's victory signalized something rather larger than a mere change in Thérèse's condition. A strange power battle had been going on within the Carmel of Lisieux, and while Thérèse herself was only on the periphery of it, she was indirectly to have an influence on its outcome. It was between the old and the new, and makes one think of nothing more than Muriel Spark and *The Abbess of Crewe*.

Marie de Gonzague had been Prioress three times, and the nuns of Lisieux were beginning to be bored with her. They were mostly women who had been brought up in the shadow of the *ancien regime*, but the spirit of the Revolution lurks deep in every French soul, and the Martin girls seemed to represent a challenge to the established order. There was the danger of a bourgeois takeover, perhaps (why precisely had they descended on Lisieux in such numbers?), but Agnes of Jesus (Pauline) seemed a good egg, and it was probably worth taking a fly on the likes of her. If you wanted to know what the future tasted like, you had to sample a morsel.

As it fell out, Marie de Gonzague was re-elected in 1896, arguing that Pauline and the Martins hardly represented a definitive new approach. However, Thérèse died in 1897, and was quickly hailed as a saint, so Pauline came back into favour again. In the new century she was made Prioress for life, Marie de Gonzague having died in 1904. The old bat had lived long enough to see herself 'replaced' by a mere bourgeois. It was a bitter if resigned end, symbolizing what was happening in the wider world. Religious life so often does.

Thérèse by an irony became very fond of Marie de Gonzague when she was out of office. This was typically perverse of her. She probably thought again of her own wilfulness and how she believed her liberty had been a peril to her, and so genuinely elevated her old *bête noire* to the position of revered guide and mentor. Marie de Gonzague had had a rough ride in the 1896 election, having to endure seven ballots before she got a clear majority. Though very ill by this time, Thérèse felt genuinely sorry for her, and wrote to console her a very curious piece called *Legend of a Very Little Lamb*.

It is a sort of fairy tale, the heroine being 'a happy shepherdess who loved her flock' (de Gonzague, by all that's unlikely). But she is given the boot by the sheep themselves, which causes her to sit on a rock and weep. A 'very little lamb' (Thérèse) thus goes to the 'heavenly pastor' (Jesus) to find out why this has happened. Jesus replies somewhat tendentiously that he has willed this particular trial – a lack of community trust – for the happy shepherdess, so that she will be strengthened and learn to depend on no one but him when the crook is once more returned to her, and she must again lead the flock.

It sounds as though Thérèse, like a floating Cardinal at a papal consistory, has been sounding out the factions and come to the conclusion that the white smoke must sooner or later waft up the chimney for Marie de Gonzague again. Thus there is the familiar old cringe in the *Legend of a Very Little Lamb*. It is more marked this time, because whatever sympathy she feels for the woman (and there is no reason to suppose it was not absolutely genuine) she realizes that obedience problems under Marie de Gonzague once again will be more than she can stomach.

Grovelling, smarmily turning away wrath, is not necessarily the action of a coward. It can be an exaggerated response in one direction for fear that a similar response in the other will lead to bloody murder. Thérèse really did not want to turn violent with Marie de Gonzague. Yet being a helpless child, a clumsy juvenile – always her sound protection in the past – did not seem quite to work with the old bat. Winsome warm smiles only hardened the frost on the other's lips. And you couldn't go on kissing the floor and pretending you liked it forever. It got wearying and made your habit filthy.

Pauline appears to have understood that Thérèse was on a short fuse, and acted accordingly. As Prioress, she lifted her sister from vulnerable dogface status to petty authority. She made her assistant Mistress of Novices.

Thérèse surprised herself, and probably the

convent as a whole, by revealing a talent for this. She had an immediate rapport with young women anxious to enter religious life – so like herself so recently – and she could understand and advise on their difficulties. She hit immediately on the non-invasive, watching and waiting technique that it often takes advisers (religious or lay as the case may be) many years to accquire:

> '... if the canvas on which an artist is working could think and speak, it obviously wouldn't be annoyed with the brush that kept on touching and retouching it: and it wouldn't be envious either, because it would know perfectly well that all its beauty came from the artist who held the brush, not from the brush itself... Well, dear Mother, I'm the poor little brush our Lord has picked out to be the means of imprinting his image on the souls which you have entrusted to me...'

It goes to show, perhaps, that in the whole of her short life, Thérèse was never called upon to demonstrate her full capacities. In the child's heart she so jealously retained there was still a deep sense of responsibility for others and an informed perception: conjoined qualities you would be lucky to find in a practising psychiatrist. Just as there is no saying what sort of tearway Thérèse might not have become had she embraced the world, so it is impossible to tell what she might not have developed into in religious life had she lived and been taken seriously.

The sad thing about her brief existence is probably that nobody ever did take it seriously.

Marie de Gonzague, when she was re-elected in 1896, turned out to be a changed woman. This was a lucky break for Thérèse. Her increasing ill-health had by now made it almost impossible for her to follow the Rule. The new Prioress at once exempted her from all taxing observances. In one respect de Gonzague remained blind, (and perhaps culpably, as we shall see), but otherwise she behaved like a concerned Mother, anxious for this child of hers who was sick.

It is time to consider Thérèse's religious vocation, and to ask whether in modern terms she could be said to have had a calling to be a Carmelite at all.

It is no doubt a contrary question to ask about a nun-saint. Yet the three vows of religion, poverty, chastity and obedience, cannot successfully (or anyway fruitfully) be assumed by a simple act of will. A charism is required: a 'call' from the Holy Spirit. Religious life is an oddity, not a norm. It has no built-in virtue save for its true devotees, and they are 'special' people: not precisely 'chosen' as some of them like to maintain, but certainly singled out from the generality.

Thérèse's difficulties with obedience may have been symptomatic of a deeper malaise, perhaps as grave as a wife's repugnance to her husband's touch in marriage. The very rigidity of her adherence to the nit-picking aspects of the Rule of Carmel shows just how hard she was finding it to conform. When you are faced with impossible demands, you can respond by either telling those riding you to drop dead, or by knuckling down and beating the system before it beats you. Successful career soldiers choose the latter course as a norm.

Thérèse did too, but there is nothing to say she could have done it for very long. Had she not died young, the short fuse would soon have burned out, and the consequent explosion would have claimed many casualties. She desperately needed to be free. Her wilfulness was not so much the fault she characterized it as, as a compulsion to declare herself before the world. Thérèse had the temperament of an artist – it is possible to see from the poems and *incunabula* how she might have practised painting or writing in another incarnation – and so was versatile and precise. But she was denied outside stimulation. The very sunshine and rain of growth and flowering, to use her own tiresome horticultural imagery, was not there.

Little children may be subjected to strict discipline, but not to the shackling of the imagination. Carmel was awfully good at that. So what Thérèse experienced in the nunnery was not so much enduring childood as stunted growth. The degree to which she had willed it on herself, of course, is another matter. The fact that it may alone have enabled her to become the most signifcant saint of modern times, the harbinger of a new spirituality, is also not the point at issue.

She simply discovered that religious life, about

which she had built up so many infantile fanatsies, was after all not the game she had initially desired to play. And it was no longer possible simply to creep away behind the bed and forget. To bury the dead birds and console yourself with melancholy. You could only leave it all to God. To God. Who can – must – draw good out of evil, sense out of foolishness, and merit and help to the world even out of the gross idiocies of a mixed-up child.

7.

Thérèse

and the

Grim Reaper

$\mathscr{A}$lmost from the moment she was born, Thérèse of Lisieux wanted to die.

It is not her most endearing characteristic. It deters many who might otherwise be attracted to and enlarged by her works and person. You gain precious little from a guru who can only tell you we're all here because, seriously, we're not all there. It cannot be really such a wash-out of a world, no matter how many Pol Pots or Iced Ts* we have to endure. Alcmena, when she learned Zeus was a native of Olympus, rejected his attentions because she felt a greater kinship with butterflies and cabbages than

---

* Pol Pot: mass murderer. Iced T: musical assassin.

with gods and signs and prodigies. It is something to do with that.

It is impossible to say how early the preoccupation with death began with Thérèse. She seems to have been a normally cheerful and gurgling baby, but almost as soon as she had left the cradle she began to understand in some strange manner that existence on this planet was a rather temporary affair, not really worth getting excited about. It was to be followed however by an everlasting 'true' life with God. You needed to get your priorities right. Concentrate on the substance rather than the shadow.

It is equally impossible to say how much of this attitude in Thérèse was conditioning and how much instinct. Plainly, Louis and Zelie would have breathed prayers over their ninth child from the day she was born, and would have imparted the tenets of the catechism to her almost as soon as she was capable of comprehending them. But for all that, there may have been something else going on at a level of which we are not aware. It is not unusual among religious people (and not necessarily those who turn out to be extremely devout) to find many who seem to have been conscious of God almost before they were conscious of themselves. Perhaps for some, in fact, the dawning of the one awareness is the dawning of the other. *Cogito ergo Deus est.*

In any event, from the time she was a toddler, mortality was on little Thérèse's mind. The first we hear of it is in a letter of Zelie's to her Visitation nun sister. Mamma seems as perplexed as she is amused:

'... Baby is such a queer little creature as you never saw: she comes up and puts her arms around me and wishes I were dead. 'Oh, poor little Mother,' she says, 'I do wish you'd die.' Then, when you scold her, she explains: 'Oh, but it's only because I want you to go to heaven: you told me yourself that one can't go to heaven without dying.' She wants to kill off her father too, when she really gets affectionate...'

Death was always just around the corner for Thérèse, and not as a dreaded loiterer. It is possible of course to say this was because she had some kind of presentiment of her own early demise, yet it was neither a morbid nor a frenzied engrossment, as it frequently is with those who have to pack a lifetime's activity into a mere fraction of the span. It was distinctly more congenial and restful. Going fishing with Louis on Sunday, she would gaze into the lazily winking river, and while he dreamed of the old man pike he must one day surely land, she would romantically envisage herself as 'an exile, longing for the eternal rest of heaven, those endless Sabbaths in our true home...'.
Everything tended to another life for her. Birds soaring into the sky were the souls of innocent children set free, the blue sky Mary's mantle to enfold them. She was a Christian Platonist, lost in her metaphysical ambiguities. 'I have never felt at home

in my body,' she once clarified. 'When I was a tiny child I was ashamed of it, and I was not comfortable in it...'

She had her first experience of death when her mother succumbed to her cancer. It was not as agreeable as she had innocently supposed, and tested all of her yet nascent faith. She stared long and hard at her mother's coffin as she lay there chalk-white and still, hating the size of it, but not crying. Zelie was now with Jesus and the angels, so it was not a crying matter. She deliberately put away from her fear and dread. Fifteen years later she stood by the coffin of an old nun, Mother Genevieve, in Carmel, this time deeply consoled. The coffin now looked quite small. Death-in-life had ceased to overshadow her.

In the influenza epidemic of 1891 three nuns died and virtually all the rest of the community took to its bed. Thérèse throughout remained on her feet, and acted happily throughout as infirmarian and mortician. Now she felt only a sort of envy for the still white corpses. The details of death remained grim and forbidding, but the thought of what stretched beyond them was enough to reconcile you to those 'accidents'.

'I've never asked God for an early death,' she once declared frankly, 'but I've always hoped this may be his will for me.' She began to dream about shuffling off the mortal coils. Her dreams in general (like the one about the devils in the garden shed) were vivid and graphic. She pre-dated the cinema, but dreamed like a scenarist. Once, as the first rays of dawn came after a restless night:

'... I was standing in a sort of gallery where several other people were present. Suddenly, without seeing how they got there, I was conscious of the presence of three Carmelite sisters... The tallest of the three figures moved towards me, and as I sank to my knees, lifted her veil, lifted it right up, I mean, and threw it over me. I recognised her without difficulty: the face was that of our Venerable Mother Anne of Jesus, who brought the reformed Carmelite order into France. There was a kind of ethereal beauty about her features, which were not radiant but transfused with light...

'I can still see the look on Mother Anne's face, her loving smile: I can still feel the touch of the kisses she gave me. And now, treated with all this tenderness, I plucked up my courage: "Please, Mother," I said, "tell me whether God means to leave me much longer on earth? Or will he come and fetch me soon?" And she, with a most gracious smile, answered: "Yes, soon. Very soon, I promise you."...'

She wanted it from the horse's mouth, and constructed the screenplay accordingly. But of course Mother Anne of Jesus, for all her venerability, might be still little more than a hand around the everlasting stables. She could have picked up unreliable information. Further assurance was needed.

It came, dramatically (and perhaps aptly) in the early hours of Good Friday 1896. Thérèse went to bed after watching till midnight on Holy Thursday at the Altar of Repose (where the Sacrament was reserved after the Maundy Mass, the main altar having been stripped and left desolate and bare). She had scarcely put her head to the pillow before she became conscious of a 'warm tide' rising up in her throat and filling her mouth. She did not know what it was, but was seized by a wild surmise:

'... my soul was flooded with joy at the thought that I was going to die: surely I must be spitting blood? Only the lamp was out, so I had to wait till morning to make certain it was all right. It wasn't a long wait: my first thought on waking was of good news coming to me, and as soon as I got to the window I realised there was no mistake. My handkerchief was soaked with blood. With an intense feeling of inward happiness, I cherished the conviction that Jesus, on the anniversary of his own death, was sending me his first summons...'

It was the kind of thrill a young girl feels on learning that her lover is at the door. The strange little detail about waiting till morning to make certain because 'the lamp was out' indicates just how much in thrall to the Rule she was. The convent was supposed to exist in darkness and silence from lights out until the hour of rising for morning office. But every good religious knows that the Rule was made for man, not man for the Rule. Thérèse thus was not in any sense obliged to be patient till morning. The truth would seem to be that she did not want check out the evidence immediately for fear of being disappointed.

Seldom can mortal illness have been greeted more joyfully. Seldom can its advances have been acknowledged more demurely. She had T.B. There was no question about that, though it is strange that no immediate medical confirmation was sought. It is also strange that nothing immediate was done about her condition. Thérèse was obliged by Rule to report her illness to the Prioress (Marie de Gonzague once more). She did this, but said she was going to tell no one else, not even her sisters, and maintained that she was in no pain, so that there was therefore no reason why she should be treated any differently from anybody else.

It was standard religious 'cool'. You were required to play down your ailments, and think of it as a fault to ask for or expect special consideration. Marie de Gonzague saw the world through the same contracting lens, and took Thérèse at her word. She did the opposite of flying into a flap, as a lesser Mother Superior might have done. She simply nodded solemn assent and allowed her subject to go about her normal tasks of prayer and work.

On that same Good Friday, Thérèse consequently finished up cleaning windows as evening closed in. She was by this time exhibiting such a ghastly pallor that a worried novice asked if she could complete the job for her. Thérèse refused. She had her passport to paradise, and her bags were packed and ready. Her business meantime was simply to get on with the job as well as she could. Death is a perfectly normal occurrence, God's affair not yours. It is certainly nothing to make a fuss about.

There are two faintly supercilious questions that must be asked about Thérèse and her illness – which as it happened remained largely untreated, and quite rapidly declined into a terminal state. Did she, in her neglect of her symptoms and disregard of general health, in fact commit suicide? And how, physically, did she manage to carry on for the best part of a year?

Thérèse had been gravely ill once before, when she was only about 10 years old. It was just after Pauline's entry into Carmel. That Easter she had begun to be afflicted with continual headaches. She did not complain much, but then Louis had to go off to Paris, and he took Marie and Léonie with him, leaving Céline and Thérèse in the charge of the Guerins. Thérèse was changing to go out with her aunt and uncle one evening, when she was overtaken by a strange fit of trembling. Soon she was shaking all over, and had to be put to bed with hot water bottles. She was no better by morning, and went into delirium.

The illness was diagnosed, apparently, but Thérèse in *L'Histoire* does not enlighten us as to what it was. She simply states that Dr Notta was called, and said that he had never heard of anybody being attacked by 'so serious a complaint so young'. The good doctor may even have thought it was incipient T.B., who knows? Anyway the illness took a grave turn, and Thérèse's life was despaired of. Thérèse however appears to have had her own ideas about things:

> 'I wish I could describe this strange illness of mine... I'm fully persuaded, now, that it was the work of the devil: but for a long time after I got well I was convinced that I had made myself ill on purpose, and that became a real torment to me...'

It was a shrewd perception, in a time of the world when not much was known about psychosomatism. But when Pauline went into Carmel, Thérèse had for the second time in her life lost her mother-figure. Psychiatrists today say you cannot do that. It was a reason to get ill, so to speak, taking a leaf out of Dr Freud's casebook (though in ignorance of the why or how of her action), Thérèse describes how she efficiently shifted the psychic bane to her hapless body:

> '... I was delirious nearly all the time and talking utter nonsense, and yet I'm quite certain I never, for a moment, lost my reason. Often I seemed to be in a dead faint, without making the slightest movement: anybody could do anything they liked with me – you could have killed me unresisting: and yet all the time I heard everything that was being said round me, and I remember it all still.

Once, for quite a long time, I couldn't open my eyes, and yet when I was left alone I opened them at once...'

Marie was horrified on returning from Paris, and at once started nursing her little sister 'with a mother's tenderness'. Thérèse, twice-bitten, resisted, giving 'endless trouble'. But then the kissing began again, and she rose from her sick bed, anxious to be sure that when Marie went out of the room she too did not vanish entirely. So today's psychiatrists do not necessarily know it all.

In any event, this was Thérèse's only experience of illness before contracting her fatal disease in Carmel. She was never robust, yet kept good health otherwise throughout her life. Her self-inflicted disorder would arguably never have killed her, because such things don't, and anyway in her deepest soul she must have known she still had a reason (as yet uncomprehended) for staying alive. But now it was different. She had never heard the word, but she knew perfectly well there was nothing psychosomatic about vomiting blood. The bridegroom was clearly 'on his way', and she was hearing the 'soft murmur' of his voice. All she wanted in her distress was for it to become louder quickly.

For a gravely sick person to take as little care of her health as Thérèse did after the first appearances of tuberculosis would probably today be considered not only foolish, but immoral. But of course there was not thought to be any cure for 'consumption' in

1896: as its nickname implies, it simply took you over and ate you up. So it was not necessarily a despairing (or for that matter brave) response to shrug your shoulders and say you would simply carry on with what you normally did for as long as you could. In the present day, unhappy AIDS victims often do the same thing.

But for all that there are certain adjustments and ameliorations to your lifestyle which you ought to make when you are seriously ill, if only out of consideration for those about you. These in Thérèse's case neither the patient herself nor Mother Marie de Gonzague (initially) seemed disposed to sanction. A sufferer from T.B. needs rest, the right food, a decent climate or at the least somewhere well-heated. The Carmel of Lisieux was damp, draughty, cold, and ill-provisioned. Thérèse was expected to adjust to Spartan conditions rather than that the least change should be made to accommodate her.

Yet it was her own will. A foot warmer was procured for her cell, mainly through the exertions of Pauline and Marie (who had been slow to catch on to the fact that she was a very sick woman, but rallied round magnificently once they did), but she virtually refused to use it. As long as she could abide by the strictures of the Rule, she pontificated (ever more weakly), she would. She believed that by accepting suffering willingly she was saving many souls, and she was determined anyway to lick that old devil of obedience that hag-rode her. Only death would finally free her, and by an irony, scrupulous observance of the dreaded Rule was bringing death closer.

It was the winter of 1896 that finally did for her. Chilled to the bone and barely able to breathe without piercing pain for the ice in the air – she muttered later that her worst physical suffering in religious life had always been the cold – Thérèse had to make a now desperately faltering way to her Prioress and gasp that she could not go on any longer. Marie de Gonzague at once responded favourably. Doctors were laid on, and treatments ordered, expense found to be no obstacle. A warm corner was prepared, a wheelchair provided, and the Martin sisters were detailed to the personal care of the youngest of their brood.

One wonders of course what kind of a game Marie de Gonzague had thought she was playing. Earlier treatment would probably not have aided Thérèse enormously, but by the time her superior got round to calling in doctors, there was nothing that could be done at all. The old bat was an old toughie. Even if Thérèse had not asked to be treated 'no differently from anybody else', it is possible that the Prioress might have acted thus anyway. After all, one came to Carmel to suffer. Everything the professed nun endured, toughed out, was for the salvation of souls.

It is another concept which eludes us today. Christians seem reluctant to believe any longer that their personal suffering is of such shining value that it can drag back souls who would otherwise slither helplessly down the greasy path to Hell. Yet it has always been accepted by the devout that prayer and sacrifice is a sort of currency. To put it at its least, things might be considerably worse if it were not for the Carmelite accepting solitude and silence in her cell, the humble toiler embracing labour for the sake of the community, the prayerful patient bearing pain cheerfully in hospital. The parable in which the kingdom is seen as the leaven in the measure of meal brings the lesson home. In spiritual terms, the few are in there pitching for the many.

But to see such 'substitution' as a kind of duty, applicable under every condition, is plainly dangerous. It is the old 'victim of divine justice' syndrome all over again. There was a venerable idea, inherited from the Fathers of the Desert (who else?), that his dedication positively obliged a monk to drag himself to prayer and penance as long as there was breath left in his body. There are stories in Rodriguez of monks dropping in their tracks between Matins and Lauds. (Better before Compline, no doubt, when their names could be immediately added to the Necrology.)

Marie de Gonzague may have yearned for the good old days of punishing penance. As we have seen it was not like that with Thérèse. Yet in practice her attitude was hardly very different. She perhaps did not seek to suffer for suffering's sake, but she was taking damn good care that there would be no chance of a miraculous recovery, as there had been with her mysterious childhood illness.

So was it suicide? The question is pejorative. There is in fact no moral obligation on anyone to prolong life when terminal conditions have been encountered. Those who routinely object to life-support machines being switched off are old-fashioned puritans. (Which is not to say there aren't cases when you wouldn't.) Thérèse in any event would have found their attitude very confusing. In a famous old example, if it is shown that the eating of oysters threatens your life, there is no obligation on you to avoid oysters. A problem might arise if you chose to eat nothing but oysters. But if you did, it would mean you had problems anyway.

To desire death, as Thérèse did all her life, is certainly not unchristian. We have not here a lasting city. However, most believers accept that they affirm the life to come more positively by a healthy and committed attitude towards this one. Progress on this earth is in some ways necessary for salvation. We are not put here merely to leave the facility in the condition in which we found it. Human history is going somewhere, though of course none of us can tell where or why. Thérèse would have found herself quite out of her depth in these waters. Yet she never pretended that her view was the right, or the only view, merely that it was hers. A child even unto mortal illness and decay, she preserved the clear, contrary insight of infancy. It was like X-ray vision. The only true reality lies behind deceptive appearances. O world invisible, we view thee.

But if she desired death, she knew nothing about

dying. Children only comprehend the end, never the means. With Marie de Gonzague as a sort of conventual Captain Hook, Peter Pan was to learn all about the awfully big adventure.

Marie de Gonzague did not precisely revert to type as Thérèse's strength and powers of resistance declined, but she began to make crashing errors of judgement. Tuberculosis is a strange malady, which even as it relentlessly destroys the sufferer, presents in such a manner as to make you believe she or he may be getting better. Thérèse, just like Marguerite Gautier (who, one sees, would hardly be the sort of model Marie de Gonzague would look to), sometimes seemed radiantly healthy. Perhaps it was on days when Thérèse looked flushed and fizzy that Marie de Gonzague formed her opinions, for she seems to have got the vague idea that the patient wasn't as sick as she was supposed to be. (The fact that, quite heroically, Thérèse would smile her little girl smile and never complain only compounded the illusion.)

But virtually all the time, she was suffering dreadfully, enduring fits of coughing that would sometimes last for hours, developing bed sores that made sitting up like being on 'spikes of iron', and fighting a savage, burning thirst, for which she could drink nothing, because liquid would only ignite worse fires within. Her tuberculosis had spread to the intestines, and a wicked internal gangrene had begun.

The convent's regular physician was a certain Dr Cornieres. As has been pointed out, there was little in the way of treatment that could be offered. Once when he was away, however, his locum by chance was Dr Neele, the man Thérèse's cousin Jeanne had married, and about whom Thérèse had consulted her when she wrote her outlandish 'Wedding Invitation'. As a relative and a younger medical practitioner, Neele was horrified by the pain Thérèse was plainly enduring, and at once ordered injections of morphia. When she heard of this, Marie de Gonzague was in her own way horrified. She was not having these new-fangled pain killers on her territory. She forbade the medication to Thérèse.

She was obviously of the school that thought God rejoiced in the cries of women in labour. Dr Cornieres returned, and supported Neele's judgement. Thérèse had worsened in the time he had been away. But De Gonzague again issued a blank refusal. Dr Cornieres therefore suggested at least syrup of morphia. But the old bat, the old toughie, allowed only – for some unfathomable reason – inhalations of ether. These in the event were worse than useless. Thérèse's breathing was so shallow that the ether could have little or no effect.

In our age, there is of course no justifying Marie de Gonzague. In her own as it happens there was still little enough. Theologians were even then rapidly coming round to the point of view that the alleviation of human suffering was a Christian duty. Post-Reformation theology generally had emphasised the need to see personal suffering as a cross sent by God to test and purify the soul. Some humbugs however developed out of that the notion that it was therefore a holy virtue to go out and seek suffering. Divines with a drop of common sense came down on the view like a ton of treatises. Now it was getting out of hand. Physical pain was in itself pretty pointless. You were only encouraged to endure it because you couldn't avoid it.

But you could avoid it with anaesthetics. It was therefore hard to make out a decent case against them, particularly when it was other peoples' pain rather than your own you were talking about. Did my neighbour's agonising cancer in any sense enlarge me? Why, come to that, had Jesus gone around relieving physical pain wherever he found it, if he actually meant the rest of us simply to grin and bear it?

On a less rarefied level, of course, the Church's approval of anaesthesia may have had something to do with the fact that elderly clerics, from whose lips dropped the pearls that the faithful snapped up, had more to gain than many others from a snappy approval of efficient painkillers. It was never put as brutally as that, but somebody well-placed theologically came quietly up with the notion that anaesthetics protected fallible mortals against 'cursing God'. (Railing against heaven as a result one's suffering was a dread of even good Christians in days when many were doomed to die in gross pain.) Nobody wanted the danger of that sort of thing, especially in a world fast turning atheist, where the railer might (unhappily, but you never knew) turn out to be a bishop or a cardinal.

As for poor Thérèse, she just suffered while the argument went on. Marie de Gonzague doubtless did not accept that a Carmelite nun was in any danger of 'cursing God'. Religious dedication, abandonment of self, meant that she might confidently look forward to grace abundant in her last agony. Thérèse would cope. The Prioress was painfully behind the times, and an atrocious death for Thérèse was the fruit of it. But she bore her pain valiantly. Here if anywhere was the 'heroic virtue' that makes saints. She had an almost miraculous resilience.

'Mother, pray for me!' she suddenly sobbed one day to Pauline. 'If you only knew how much I am suffering. Ask that I may not lose patience... And I so longed for martyrdom of every kind! One has to experience it to know what it means...'

But then, a day later, exhausted, in less acute pain, more reflective: 'I could never ask greater sufferings of God. Yet if he were to increase them I should endure them gladly, because they would be of his sending... But if I were to ask for them they would be all my own, and I should have to bear them all alone: and I have never been able to do anything all by myself...'

And finally, more darkly, after another sleepless night of meaningless agony:

'... I can quite well understand that people without faith commit suicide when they are in such great pain. Take care you do not leave any poisonous medicines beside the sick when they are attacked by such violent pain. I tell you that when one is suffering like this, one is but a step removed from going out of one's mind...'

Euthanasia, a suicide more deliberate than the one she may in her way already have been consenting to, seems to have crossed her mind. The game was up, but it was not over and it would not end. There was an appealing logic for her in thinking perhaps she could take matters into her own hands. She certainly did not blame anyone who did. Her prayers, one feels, resound down the years for wretched humans abandoned to nothing but their own resources. She was of their number in her last hours. She had at length, despite all her protestations of dependence and helplessness, come to believe that she was hopelessly, helplessly on her own. God had deserted her.

It is par for the course with the saintly, of course. *My God, my God, why have you forsaken me...?* rings around every holy deathbed like the passing bell. Nor did Thérèse's darkness descend on her suddenly and without warning. It had been growing for some time, finally thickening to blackest pitch as her physical sufferings became intolerable. How could God let her suffer like this? Who was this lover, this bridegroom, to stand by doing nothing while the object of his affections lay writhing in agony?

She had prefigured her last state of mind – despair in all but intention – earlier, ironically enough in the section of *L'Histoire* addressed to Marie de Gonzague. She confesses in a moving passage:

'... I get tired of the darkness all around me, and try to refresh my jaded spirits with the thoughts of that bright country where my hopes lie. Yet what happens? It is a worse torment that ever: the darkness seems to borrow, from the sinners who live in it, the gift of speech.

'I hear its mocking accents: "It's all a dream, this talk of a heavenly country, bathed in light, scented with delicious perfumes, and of a God who made it all, who is to be your possession in eternity! You really believe, do you, that the mist which hangs about you will clear away later on? All right, all right, go on longing for death ! But death will make a nonsense of your hopes ; it will only mean a night darker than ever, the night of mere non-existence."...'

Perhaps then, at the very end, it was a sort of fear that kept her alive. She clung to the frail, slithery spar of faith in the wild shipwreck of doubt, and that takes huge resolve and determination. Hope had to return to her before she could die. It is amazing how long she hung on, considering that eventually she could eat nothing, could barely sleep, hardly knew where she was, and could not understand why she continued to live. She must have been, so unusually for her, terrified. Death, so long desired, was after all just a grinning old skull swathed in black.

Her sisters, both natural and religious, did not help much. The religious ones were so concerned for her that they managed (as only the truly virtuous can) never to give her a moment's peace. She could not even suffer alone. Pauline and Céline meantime had woken up to the fact that their sister was a saint – it had been Thérèse's assessment of herself too, as we have learned, but it was arguably at the end the thing furthest from her mind – and so they were taking down her every last *aperçu*.

Many of them were simply not worth recording. There is hardly much point in having it scrupulously noted down that once, overtaken by mild delirium no doubt, you waved a shaky hand at a glass of vile medicine that looked like an after-dinner liqueur, and croaked 'There you have a figure of my life... People have always thought that I was quaffing delicious liqueurs, while it was bitterness, bitterness all the time...'

The precise end took its time in coming. Faint comedy creeps into the script here. The Carmelite Rule requires the community to gather at the deathbed of a dying sister, but it was not clear just when exactly Thérèse was perishing. Thus there were a number of false alarms. The nuns were summoned on a couple of occasions, but then dismissed again. Thérèse herself became puzzled and even faintly annoyed. 'How does one die?' she plaintively gasped to Marie de Gonzague one morning when she came round.

Thérèse must in fact have had an enviable constitution and a strong heart. It only had to stop pumping, after all, for her to be free of her excruciating pain and incipient despair. But it did not for quite some time. Thérèse endured a long passion. Eighteen months separated the first evidence of illness from the last breath, and the last six of them were months of increasing agony.

The end came at about 7 p.m. on the evening of 30 September 1897. About an hour before, Thérèse had muttered through her death rattle, as though ending some long debate within herself, '...well, after all, I would not choose to suffer less...' No more was heard on the theme. As 7 o'clock drew close, she looked at the crucifix and was heard to breathe 'I love him... my God, I love you...'

Then she slumped back on her pillows: but a moment later sat bolt upright once more. Her gaze was fixed on a statue of our Lady. Her expression changed, as though she suddenly perceived something so astonishing and out of the ordinary as to be unbelievable. It only lasted a moment: then she fell back dead. Her death mask was a mask of perfect peace and joy.

It is this final aspect of Thérèse that perhaps haunts most tellingly. It is this last image of the everlasting little girl staring spellbound into the vault of eternity that will not go away.

So she stares for all of us, still, inviting us to share her innocent wonder: at life, the world, creation with its beauties, suffering and death, the wonders beyond. She testifies to a wholeness of existence, a unity between the here and the hereafter such as many of us may once have perceived when we were seven years old, but have not clapped tired old adult eyes on since.

We are afraid to look again, of course, because what we see anew make old claims on us. And that is why she stands, staring, staring. She is a thoroughly annoying kid. A Doctor of the Church at last, she can still only express herself in nursery language, and does not intend to change. She will force us to share her amazingly simple vision sooner or later.

She will lead us back to innocence.